C000201904

The Trouble with

Pink Wheelbarrows:

Insight, Inspiration, and Ideas

for Budding Entrepreneurs

by

Sam Eaton

The Trouble With Pink Wheelbarrows

© 2022 Sam Eaton
All rights reserved. No part of this publication may be reproduced, distributed, or transmitted in any form or by any means, including photocopying, recording, or other electronic or mechanical methods, without the prior written permission of the publisher, except in the case of brief quotations embodied in critical reviews and certain other noncommercial uses permitted by copyright law. For permission requests, write to the publisher, addressed "Attention: Permissions Coordinator:" at the address below:

Sam Eaton
England
Sam@Mindabilityconsulting.org

Ordering Information:
Special discounts are available on quantity purchases by corporations, associations, educational institutions, and others. For details, contact Sam Eaton above.
Printed in the United States of America
First Edition
Softcover ISBN 978-1-5136-9780-2
Hardcover ISBN 978-1-5136-9756-7
Ebook ISBN 978-1-5136-9781-9

Publisher
Winsome Entertainment Group LLC

Acknowledgements

There's a saying that 'it takes a village to raise a child', I also believe the same is true of successful businesses and big projects. In most instances, they are the brainchild or idea of one individual. To bring them to life, requires a great team of experts.

I am so grateful to dear friends like Jen Coken and Barbie Winterbottom who helped with this book. To people I consider friends and mentors, Tracie Sponenberg, and Steve Cadigan. Thank you for all for your ongoing support and belief in what I am trying to achieve. Thank you for all the great things you are doing! To Jill and Barfie, for always being a phone call away, your patience and friendship never ceases to astound and humble me.

I'd like to thank my fabulous team, Caroline Somer, founder of Somer Design who produced our book cover, for believing in me, for uplifting me and for giving me the support I so needed. To Jack – for being such an integral part of MindAbility and for all that you do – I have never and will never take it for granted, your voice and opinions matter to me.

Lastly and by no means least, my thanks, gratitude and love go to my husband, Clint. For having faith in me, even during those times when I've lost faith in myself. I am fortunate to have found you and thank you for all you do.

My Personal Journey

My dad had a handful of philosophies that he lived his life by. A couple of them have really stuck with me. Firstly, always remember that the most successful person in any room is actually the biggest failure.

Why is that? Well, they've had more "nos" than anyone else throughout their lives and are comfortable with that.

Secondly, when you're thinking of launching and building a successful business, throw your ego down the toilet. Literally. His belief was that if you weren't prepared to clean toilets, then you shouldn't be a businessowner. Don't get me wrong—I'm not saying that those who are janitors are any less valued than business owners. In fact, quite the opposite. His point was that if you want to run any business, and run it well, you leave your ego at the door. Period.

By contrast, my mum instilled in us that every person was loved by someone, somewhere. What right does any one person have to criticise, be unreasonable, or judge them? Perhaps we should ponder on that point for a moment longer in today's confused world, eh?

I distinctly remember being a child sitting in the car in a long line of traffic waiting to catch a ferry. I can't for the life of me remember what had gone wrong, but I do recall there were delays and we missed our original ferry crossing to the Channel Islands. Stressed out to the max, my dad took umbrage with one of the ferry port's staff—and it wasn't pretty. Hence my mum's point about being reasonable.

Dad's business career was impressive. He built up a huge business, from scratch, without any financial support or loans from anyone. He was the definition of self-made. He was also a very modest man, with energy that could power a nuclear power station and a drive that came from providing for his family and building a better life for his children. He wasn't afraid of anyone or anything and was always planning how he could win his next big contract.

He always encouraged us to explore and experience new things, to give something a go, even if we were slightly unsure of it. So as a little girl aged nine, I tried my hand at my first business and thought I could grow and sell small fir trees .... oh, and tiger lilies.

Dad's main business was in safety surfacing, and, at one point, he had over sixty-five people on the payroll. His team loved him, slightly feared him, and most importantly, respected him. Mum always proudly tells the story (of which there are many) of the time when Dad had a contract on a war ship. The captain of the ship had come out and asked if he could speak to the "governor." My dad replied that he wasn't there, and could he pass a message on? The message was simple: the captain wanted to congratulate the men and tell the boss how impressed he was with their work ethic. Dad thanked him and got back to the job, with his men.

There are times in my career when I did let ego get the better of me, and when it did, I always self-corrected by going back to that story that Mum was so proud of and I remain proud of today.

I've never been academically bright—in fact, I was distinctly average. I had to really work hard to get the grades I got before going off to technical college where I trained as a bilingual secretary. Everything we were taught, from touch typing to shorthand, we learned in English and French.

I had the arrogance of an exuberant, bubbly, and fun-loving teenager and had HUGE plans. At that stage, I had it all mapped out. I'd get a job in the diplomatic core, potentially with The Foreign Office, work my way up and use this as my ticket to work all over the world. That plan was scuppered at the first hurdle. Turns out that I wasn't as diplomatic as I'd thought. So that one was off the table.

My first job was working for KPMG, where I started off in the typing pool. I met a fabulous bunch of girls and became great friends with one of the young girls, Charlotte, and one gnarly, delightful, East End older lady called Sue, who has taught me one of the biggest lessons of all in life. She once told me, "Girl, just remember, everyone takes a s***, so if you ever feel intimidated by someone, just remember that." Amazing the dreadful image this can conjure up.

3

Charlotte and I took London by storm together, and in fact, we shared a flat together in Battersea. I remember those days fondly. However, after eighteen months, I decided it was time to move on. Little did I know what was in store for me.

After passing all the tests that any recruiter required before putting a candidate forward, I got a call for an interview at Goldman Sachs, which was based in Fleet Street at the time, in the old Telegraph building.

I walked through the doors at Peterborough Court, the address of Goldman Sachs, and was taken aback at the vast steel pillars and the acres of black marble ahead of me to get to the very smart and stern looking receptionists. I was dispatched up to the top floor of the building to a meeting room and told to wait. My future boss walked through the door. He was one of the top seven men in Wall Street, which I later found out, and destined for the top at Goldman. I was twenty years of age.

I initially started off as his "Number 2 PA" and worked for him for almost two years. The hours were horrific. I had a pager that turned off only between 1am and 5am, seven days a week. Gruelling.

Needless to say, I learned A LOT in a very short amount of time and built up my resilience like you wouldn't believe. His office was like something out of *The Devil Wears Prada* (to give you a sense of the opulence and trepidation people felt when they were summoned). In fact, I often joke to friends and family that I swear the set of that film was based on his office. Everything had to be perfect, and I mean EVERYTHING. Down to a phone number (which I realise is critical when you need to return a call.) Mistakes weren't tolerated. You could make a lot of money, and I did. It wasn't real life, though. I celebrated my twenty-first birthday in London, New York, and Paris. God, looking back at that person, I was obnoxious as hell.

I was almost twenty-two when, after one fateful altercation, it was game over for me. Within three days of this row, I was recruited by the CEO of BSkyB's office, Sam Chisholm. He changed my path forever, and I will be forever grateful for his guidance, even though he provided it in his own inimitable style.

Again, I started in that role as his Number 2 PA. It was fun—long hours, complex, and outrageous. BSB had just merged with BSkyB—we had a lot to prove and a huge sense of hope. Sam recruited an incredible team around him, and BSkyB created history in the UK. Record sports deals, set top boxes, and my goodness, so much else.

I stayed with Sam until he left Sky. He was such a support to me. I didn't want to stay in Sky, however. I was keen to branch out to public relations, having worked with Sam in this area as part of my role. I was dispatched to British Interactive Broadcasting and became the press officer that launched interactive television around the UK.

For those in the UK who might remember it, we took a giant sofa all around the UK for three months to show people what interactive television was all about. It was an incredible experience. Flying into Belfast with the ex-Head of Communications for Department of Media Culture and Sport was eye-opening.

I had a brief spell at Weber Shandwick, until we parted company. At that point, I set up my first business and went into partnership with a great friend to provide public relation services to clients all around the UK. We had a delightful time—far too much fun in fact. We won a lot of work despite ourselves.

From there, I moved out of London and continued to build the business on my own, and it grew to have quite a reputation. Cue the first of three marriages. This one was short-lived. I was twenty-seven, and all of my friends were settling down and getting married. I wanted to fit in. I wanted my own husband, home, the 2.4 kids, and the golden retriever who bounded up to you when you got home.

Turns out I still had a lot of growing up to do. I could hold down impressive jobs, build businesses, but I'd devoted little to no time to my own development. This breakup caused many problems... not with my first husband, but with people who knew us. I was a workaholic at this point and had two companies. One was the PR business and the second was a flooring business that I was building up with my father. I would regularly work the PR business during the day

6

and drove to a job I'd sold to act as the H&S officer in the evening for contracts on the flooring side.

I got lonely and secretly went online and had a few dates. At around this time, I was being invited to give keynote speeches all over the country. I met a fabulous company called Sitelynx whilst in Liverpool and went to work for them for several very happy years in a business development capacity. We won some major contracts whilst I was there.

My loneliness got the better of me and I ultimately met and married husband number two and moved to the West Country. During that time, I took a directorship at another digital marketing agency and helped build that up to be award-winning. I finally resigned and set up my own digital marketing agency and worked with an historic client whilst winning new clients—rapidly. The business seemed to be an overnight success; however, my marriage to a toxic partner was falling apart. All I will say on this matter is that it came to an aggressive end, for which I received treatment for PTSD for over a year.

Despite the trauma of my personal life, I stayed with that business for over a decade and helped build that from a small team of five to a business with over twelve staff and a £4M turnover. It was an HR consultancy. I fell in love with HR. Before joining, I had no idea the impact that meaningful HR could have on a company, or the risks that business owners unwittingly take when they don't hire HR.

I took it upon myself to focus on my development. I studied gender diversity in a short course at Insead, read as many books on HR, people development, organisational development as I could, and followed HR leaders and challengers in the field on LinkedIn as I continued to grow my own reputation.

I was determined to "do single" well this time. I learnt Italian and rented the most idyllic tiny cottage you can think of. It seemed to have a life of its own and was a living and breathing thing. I've never lived anywhere quite like it. I was at the gym at least three to four times a week, and my Saturday mornings comprised of one-hour spin class followed by a one-hour combat class.

Eventually, one bright Sunday morning, my dear friends had arranged for a friend of theirs to watch us take part in a short fun run. Unfortunately, suffering from a hangover and feeling a bit of a chesty cough before turning up at the fun run, I had accidentally taken a swig of surgical spirit instead of cough mixture. I will NEVER forget that burning sensation. For anyone who doesn't know what surgical spirit is, it's a strong disinfectant product that I always had to keep my ear-rings clean.

You can imagine I turned up at the race completely green, bleary-eyed, and thoroughly disenchanted, but I couldn't let my friends down. That friend they invited? Well, that relationship developed quickly, and we bought a house together as we quickly wanted to start a family. That wasn't to be. On the day of my parents' golden anniversary, he left the house and never came back. He died dramatically, as it turns out, from a heart attack.

I was back at work one month after he died, the post-mortem, the legal challenges (as we weren't married), the funeral. Of course, I wasn't ready to go back, and my work suffered. A colleague gave me a piece of feedback that created such a fire within me I knew I had to change the course of my life.

I'd been caring far too much about others' opinions. We've all been there, right? I wanted to be completely selfish, find my path. I guess I could turn into a caricature of myself and be a life coach, right? This is how NOT to do it in your personal life. But I'm a commercial beast, through and through. I'm great at building B2B businesses.

One more consultancy gig after that and then 23 March 2020—the world changed. On my birthday. Now my birthday is also the day that we went into our first lockdown.

But, I saw a HUGE opportunity: if people didn't need my services and expertise as a business coach during a period where the world was starting to go through one of its biggest changes in our lifetime, then when would be a good time?

The world of HR started to go through accelerated changes. There was, and still remains, NO rule book. That's a good thing, however, because consultancy founders and solopreneurs were looking for programmes and support that could help them navigate, plan, and grow their businesses through such uncertainty.

MindAbility was born, and we are now into our second year. We've worked with companies across the UK, USA, Canada, and South Africa. I've been bowled over both by how tough it's been in this climate and the opportunities that are here.

Several months before the lockdown and after I'd moved again to re-establish myself, my closest friends nagged me to start dating again. Why on earth would I want to do something that ridiculous after everything I had been through? Anyway, after much nagging, I came up with a cunning plan. I signed up to Bumble, which is the dating app where women reach out to men they quite like. My plan was to sit at home on a Friday night, swipe left a few times, have a couple of conversations from the safety of my sofa without the hassle of actually having to date someone, and then tell my wonderfully concerned friends that I was dating. What could possibly go wrong?

Trouble was, on my very first day on the app, a face appeared in front of me that I could not resist. We met within a couple of weeks of our first conversation, had a wonderful lunch in a small country pub, and talked for hours. Our relationship flourished and developed very quickly through lockdown and all that followed. We've followed our path together, and he has been incredibly supportive of me, my mission, and the business, even from our early days of being together.

We both knew that MindAbility would be a success. It was a collective hunch and somehow has turned into our vision. Today, he is my husband, my island of happiness, and my Boo.

What on earth has all of this to do with the title of this book *The Trouble with Pink Wheelbarrows*? Well, this book is written for any ambitious entrepreneur, trying to find their way and learn from others who have built successful businesses. I've broken it down into three parts, which we do in our coaching programmes. Those parts are defined as EMPOWER, CREATE, and SUCCEED.

Over the next three sections, I will share insights from interviews with founders all over the world that will help you to EMPOWER who you are and what you do, to CREATE the success you desire, and to SUCCEED.

We aren't just going to talk about the "what." That can be so frustrating. You want to know more about the "how," right? You will get plenty of insights into the "how" to help guide you as build your business.

"Oh my goodness, another coach," I hear you cry. 'Fraid so. Having built five businesses, I'm most proud of my biggest failure, an online retail store. I will forever be haunted by the fact that one Christmas my home was overrun with pink wheelbarrows. Out of all our stock, the damn pink wheelbarrows were one of a handful of products we simply couldn't order in fast enough. I quickly found out that packing them for distribution was even more of a nightmare. But I learned, and now you can learn from my failures.

The one last thing I'd say is enjoy the ride as you build your business. You are going to have good days, and boy are you going to have bad. Don't wish it away—you'll be surprised at how fast time seems to go. It will all be worth it. Keep a note somewhere of all your small wins. You will be pleasantly surprised as you look back at just how far you progress each day, week, month, and eventually years. Remember, success is not a destination. It is a journey.

Part 1:

Empower

1

The Meaning of Empowerment

"The goal is to grow so strong on the inside that nothing on the outside can affect your inner wellness without your conscious permission."
~Homebody Club

EMPOWER—WHAT DOES IT MEAN?

noun

1. authority or power given to someone to do something.
   "individuals are given empowerment to create their own dwellings"
   o the process of becoming stronger and more confident, especially in controlling one's life and claiming one's rights.
   "political steps for the empowerment of women"

'The process of becoming stronger and more confident.' Sounds quite cold, doesn't it? Frankly, the definition makes it sound far too easy for my liking. You don't just pop out to your local grocery store or supermarket and find a bit of empowerment off the shelf and make it okay. It takes a lot of hard work to feel empowered. That still doesn't answer the question of what it means.

Based on my experience, empowerment is the ability to be comfortable to speak out and speak up. To have the ability to admit when things don't go your way and your own accountability in that.

Empowerment is also about being comfortable with the mistakes we have made and gaining an understanding from that. It's one of the many ways in which we learn; therefore, making mistakes actually empowers us.

It's one of those mistakes that has inspired me to write this book.

2

The Pink Wheelbarrow Story

"When you boil it down, a book title is a business decision."
~Bethany Atazadeh

Many years ago, a budding psychology student asked me to draw a picture of my ideal house. Frankly, I find it hard to draw a snowman, so I wasn't too enamoured with the task. However, I was curious and started to draw.

I drew a house with a fluffy tree to the side of it, flowers in the front garden, and birds in the sky, which were obviously upside-down M's. Like I said, drawing most certainly isn't my forte.

Apparently, my drawing was a cause for concern. It symbolized that I didn't see boundaries, nor did I recognise them. *Where's the harm in that*? I thought. Turns out that many of the mistakes I've made in my life have resulted from lack of boundaries and my sheer ambition.

So, what does this have to do with pink wheelbarrows?

Online retail, how hard could it be? After all, I love shopping. It's a hobby and not a chore. Combining my love of shopping and gardening was going to be my ticket to extreme wealth. Oh, how wrong can you be?

How much stock would we need to hold? How did we really know what the demand would be? These were all questions that needed scalable plans behind them. Luckily, my two business partners and investors ran a business that sold product, and lots of it, all across Europe.

The trick in life, and with anything, is always in the preparation. I'm not the most patient of people, but I do recognise the need to plan, plan, and then plan some more. One of the many philosophies that my dad shared with me and that I abide by today is to plan for the worst and hope for the best. Being mindful of that when researching the viability of any new venture is critical.

We identified an opportunity to sell high-quality gardening products and started off with a select line, including handheld gardening tools, kneeling pads that you could have napped on, gardening aprons, pots, storage tins of different sizes and colours with "compost," "plant labellers," and "seed packets" written across them. All the things that you never realised you needed until you saw them. You get the picture?

After several months of trading, we were fast approaching Christmas. For a small business such as ours, we got stock in from late August for our demand. Attending the trade shows to identify our stock and negotiate pricing was an eye-opener. Competition was fierce across the garden retail sector. It was around the time where gardening was just becoming cool, and we were being encouraged to create our own green space, even if it was just a plant pot on a balcony.

November came and we started to see a huge increase in customers buying things like tin containers for compost. Our outrageously expensive gardening gloves, aprons, and kneeling pads were also flying off the shelves before Christmas.

But what we needed was novelty. This is where the pink wheelbarrows came in. I convinced my partners that they would be a good idea as they were fairly expensive and we'd gotten a great deal on them from our wholesalers.

When we were negotiating, we couldn't work out why they weren't selling well via the wholesalers. After all, they were a bit different and an ideal Christmas present for the budging gardener.

The order went in, and it was decided that we'd distribute the wheelbarrows amongst our houses and outbuildings. This is where the plan started to fail. Even writing this, I'm thinking, "How on earth did I see this as a good idea? Should I stop writing IMMEDIATELY and make out like I'm a huge success all round?" But honestly, what good would that do, eh? I'd be lying to myself and to you.

At the time, I lived in a small house overlooking a lazy brook, which drifted below a small bridge at the end of our row of houses. The quiet, tranquil scene was rudely awoken by the continuous torrent of pink wheelbarrows being delivered to my house by large courier lorries—you know, the really big ones that are noisy and most certainly shouldn't be going down quiet country lanes. As with a tide, there were ebbs and flows of said trucks turning up and product being wheeled across multiple households to get to mine.

However, the undercurrents were something else.

Try packing a wheelbarrow for delivery after committing to providing it gift-wrapped. We couldn't get boxes in quick enough, nor could we find alternatives. In our haste, I wrapped them with brown paper, added a bow, and dispatched them.

It was time-consuming and space-consuming, taking up most of my living room as we were trying to save costs. This caused friction on the home front.

What did I learn? I didn't know the first thing about the online retail world, or in fact the B2C (Business to Consumer) world.

If I factored my time into picking up the wheelbarrows from my partners, getting them wrapped, coordinating deliveries—we lost money.

The maddening part of it all was that our compost tins and those damned pink wheelbarrows were our best sellers. More work, more stress, and more hassle.

We continued to trade, we continued to analyse and forecast forward, and I'm glad we did that. We simply didn't have the available capital to invest in areas of marketing that were badly needed to generate the revenue we had anticipated.

Winding the business up with stock AND capital was the right thing to do. Did it feel like a failure? Of course it did. Like anyone, I hate losing. I learned a long time ago that it's no good beating yourself up about these things. Rather, learn from it, learn what you're good at, and more importantly, what you're not.

I've always been ambitious—ridiculously ambitious, in fact. How could I do it better, quicker, and faster than anyone else? I learned many valuable lessons, one of which was to manage my impatience.

Today, I start most of my talks with the opening line of "Have you ever had to deal with pink wheelbarrows? They have been my greatest failure. As a result, it turns out those moments of sheer frustration and the odd tear shed in sheer agitation were the best things that could have ever happened to me."

If I were to draw that house again? I think I'd put a small picket fence around the front of it. That fence would depict the fact that I have a better understanding of my limitations.

3

Know Thyself

"I knew that if I failed, I wouldn't regret that,
but I knew the one thing I might regret is not trying."
~Jeff Bezos, founder and CEO Amazon

Really. Know what you are good at.

How do you know what you are good at if you haven't developed the skills or mindset yet? How can we ever truly know ourselves and what we are capable of?

I'm closer to fifty than I am forty, which isn't something I'm particularly happy about, if I'm honest. My forty-plus years on this planet have taught me one thing: we are complex beings, and those of us who are curious about people will always strive to know ourselves.

There are people out there who are far better at it than me—a fairly obvious statement considering my collection of failed marriages and a comment made by my mum that had such an impact. In a fit of pique (and well-deserved, by the way), she explained, "You need to stop being such a rolling stone. You need to learn to settle."

Initially that stung, and I spent mere moments trying to justify myself in my mind before I stopped in my tracks and my inner self kicked in. I am relentless, which makes me restless and always curious. That is who I am. Life is short, and I want to experience as much of life and the world as I can, on my terms.

But how does this relate to the business world? It's actually the root of many small business owners' problems.

How often have you read or heard a founder/small business owner say "I want to make a difference." Or "We are different from anyone else." In fact, there are over 14,700,000 businesses that all claim that they want to make a difference. It begs the question, "Make a difference in what?"

Let's look at it another way: according to a report by Intuit, it predicted seventeen million new small businesses would be formed in 2022 in the US.

So how can they all be different? The fact of the matter is that it's hard to create what was previously known as a 'unique selling proposition' in today's competitive world. The rise of personal brands has created even greater competition.

Know thyself means understanding your own limitations, and be very, very clear on the benefits or outcomes that your business offers. Let me give you an example.

Vine used to be a video hosting social media website, giving its users the ability to create six-second sharable videos. They've been described as trying to be YouTube vlogs. Twitter had been building its reputation as a microblogging site.

When Twitter purchased Vine, it made a lot of sense, giving Twitter the opportunity to try and compete with the likes of the big social media beasts like Facebook on their video content.

Sadly, Vine's existence was short-lived, formed in 2012 and closed in 2017. It died because it became unprofitable and failed to meet its market's needs. It stuck to what it wanted to do, rather than what the market wanted.

Firstly, they didn't budge on their six-second length. Content creators want to experiment and try different forms of short video, but they weren't given the opportunity to do so. On that note of keeping their target audience engaged, Vine couldn't help content creators to monetize their content because the window they had was too small—six seconds.

There were many other problems that poor Vine had to contend with, which certainly didn't help. They were a great company with a great idea, but it's a classic example of an organisation that had a great idea and continued to develop their idea on their terms whilst failing to understand the wants and needs of its audience.

Having worked with many HR consultancy and people founders around the world over the last twelve to eighteen months, the common mistake I have seen is business owners wanting to offer their services with little thought for what their clients *actually want and need*.

That's the key to all of this. By asking some pretty basic questions, you can quickly get to an understanding of who you want to work with and what they want.

Who are you? Are you clear on what you offer and *how* your offering impacts your prospects? By that, do you understand the *outcome* that your work will have on your clients?

Now let's look at your potential clients. Does your offering benefit their wants and needs? Have you spoken to people in your network who fit the profile of the kind of clients that you want to work with?

Sometimes, it's the most obvious things that we can miss when we are building a business. There's just so much to do. On that point, don't overthink it. Start selling one proposition, sell it well, get good at it, and build your confidence in your sales pitch, delivery, and closing.

We're in the era of personal brands. With real focus, individuals and small businesses can build their reputations—and solid ones at that—in less than eighteen months. People need to see you 'around' regular posts on LinkedIn, sharing your knowledge with vibrancy and humour. That always seems to work.

EXERCISE

In this chapter, we talked about having a clear understanding of your clients' wants and needs, which is essential. The two aren't always the same.

Take some time to think about the following questions:

1. What do you *think* your client wants?

2. What do they want?

3. How does that differ from what they need?

4. What are the gaps (if any) between what you want to sell them and what they want to buy from you?

4

Trouble with Ego

"Embrace what you don't know, especially in the beginning, because what you don't know can become your greatest asset. It ensures that you will absolutely be doing things different from everybody else."
~Sara Blakely, founder SPANX

We need to have confidence in our own ability without having an oversized ego. There is a fine line, believe it or not. Let me explain. By the way, this is simply my take and what I've observed over the years.

Running your own business is not easy. Please don't let anyone lull you into a false sense of security that there is a steady upward trajectory and that it will be all right. That's not always the case. We need to have an unwavering belief in what we are doing to succeed. That belief will get us through those dark days when we are too tired to get up or we almost feel toxic inside ourselves because of the crazy hours we are working. That unwavering belief is the thing that keeps us going and focused. In my mind, that's confidence.

I remember when I set up MindAbility, I had a plethora of people who thought I was absolutely mad to set up the business. "There are too many coaches out there already," booed the naysayers. The worst one I heard was "I think you are absolutely mad. I bet you'll be looking for a job in six months' time." Needless to say, I no longer talk to the person who spewed out those last words.

So why is there such a fine line between ego and confidence? Ego is defined as "a person's sense of self-esteem or self-importance." If that's overinflated to the point of ignoring the facts, well, frankly, bad things can happen.

Fresh out of tech college, I skipped over to Paris, where I just KNEW I'd make my dreams come true. What could possibly go wrong? I was a bilingual secretary. I could dream in French as well as English and I was an ambitious and hardworking Brit.

I got a job in a local council for a few months and started to teach piano lessons on the side to earn some extra cash. I lived about forty-five minutes outside of Paris with a family as the rents were extortionate.

For six months, I attempted to 'make it big.' What on earth was I thinking? I was still a teenager, with no experience whatsoever, not a penny to my name, and an ego the size of, well, the aeroplane that flew me out there, if I'm honest.

I returned to England, tail very firmly tucked between my legs, and hunkered down. I got a job in a typing pool at KPMG. Within a year of that job and all the fun and frolics that came with it, I joined Goldman Sachs, working for one of Wall Street's finest.

There I experienced some of the biggest egos that I have ever witnessed in my lifetime. My biggest lesson? I saw exactly how NOT to be. How NOT to treat people. The repercussions that toxic and bullying behaviour can have on individuals are extreme. I also witnessed the bizarre and sometimes cruel clashes between those with equally large egos.

Interlude

An Interview with Tiffany Castagno

The word "empower" is overused on a regularly basis, and it's lost its powerful intention. To empower is huge, and, as small business owners, we all need that.

You know those days where all you want to do is eat crap, watch TV, sleep all day, or just do ANYTHING but work? We've all had them. We will all continue to have those days and that's okay. Most of the time, it's our body and mind telling us that we need to take care of ourselves.

I was talking to one of our first ever clients the other week and we discussed the need to surround yourself with inspirational business leaders, those who are putting the work in and take the time to empower others.

Whilst planning this book, I wanted the voices of other inspirational business leaders to be heard, so I decided to interview a bunch of them to share their journey, their highs and lows—and the advice they would give someone like you.

I would never have met Tiffany Castagno if it hadn't been for Linke-dIn. In fact, most of my interviewees I met on the platform. Many have become dear friends, and I have been inspired by their wisdom, their positivity, their pragmatism, and their ability to empower and inspire.

Tiffany is the founder of CEPHR and has built up an impressive business in just two years. She is all about transformative HR and has been described as the Curator of Culture. She's not afraid to challenge the status quo and has helped many businesses to scale and change their models to adapt to today's challenging trading conditions.

When she's not working hard on her business, she has numerous volunteering roles, such as AscenderPGH, which is a vibrant hub with educational programs for entrepreneurs, mentorship, expert coaching, and incubation to encourage innovation and growth for fledgling businesses in the Pittsburgh area. She is also on the Board of Directors for Open Field, who are on a mission to improve the lives and futures of youth through sport by promoting health, education, leadership, and life skills through soccer. I could go on, but you get the picture, right? This lady is the epitome of empowerment!

When Tiffany first started her business in the midst of the chaos of 2020, she faced significant adversity. Business owners were shutting their doors, having staffing issues, struggling to make it.

TIFFANY:

"What have I gotten myself into? It was supposed to be my side hustle while I was looking for a new opportunity. I figured I could help some folks out, get some money, and just be self-sustaining. And I ended up being so impactful to people that they started making referrals. My own business grew, and employers realized they really could pay more attention to their employees."

In my work it's important to empower my leader (client). When clients work with an HR consultant, most of them have never done it before. They don't know what that means. They're not sure of what lies in the HR wheelhouse. They don't know that they can be empowered. And so that's part of my role too.

Not only to help support them through building out their infrastructures and helping them scale and making sure they're engaging, leading, and retaining their employees, but also to empower them as leaders to be able to say, "Okay, I do have this possibility. I can think about this strategically." And part of that is making sure that they're not reactive, that they really understand how to build a program from the ground up, how to message it appropriately, that they feel empowered to not have me be the go-between.

When these light bulbs go off, it's just fascinating. I do that to empower them through a co-create process that empowers me because I now feel like, "Hey, I'm giving them a pathway. I'm helping them see around the corners that they maybe can't."

But then I feel empowered because I know I'm making an impact, helping them help their employees, their clients, other stakeholders, the community. And that, for me, is super impactful.

Just learning from all the bumps along the way. It's been so bumpy, and I'm learning so much all the time.

And that's a lot of stress and pressure at times, but it's so liberating. And so empowering to know, "Hey, I built this, this thing is growing, and there are opportunities to constantly build it better for myself and my clients." It's been such a whirlwind learning how to give myself grace and space, not to be like necessarily tied to the business.

I think we feel like we have to be so connected and we go, go, go, and there's this hustle culture. We forget to take that time away so that we're not burning out. That mental health component is a huge piece of empowerment as a business owner, especially as a small business owner.

SAM:

This is such a timely topic because I just came across something on LinkedIn late last week about how the face of HR is changing. I saw a New York Times article titled "Your New Head of HR" that made the comparison that HR is now akin to the school nurse. That resonated with me because all the things that have changed over the last two years were being tapped into, from clients, from our employees, to being able to know how this is shifting. There is a human impact to that.

What happens is people start thinking, "Oh wait, there's more to it than me, just this regulation. How does that actually apply to my employees?" And so from an HR perspective, we are running at a pace faster than ever.

We are tasked with being more compliance heavy than ever because of these shifting guidelines. It's quite a whirlwind.

TIFFANY:

I have my own thoughts and feelings about how safe it is out there in the world and what that looks like. And then, to try to be objective enough to not impose my own thoughts and perspectives on my clients, but to really look at what it means for their particular business and workplace, because they're all in different industries.

SAM:

As you can see, Tiffany works really hard, daily in fact, on being present in her own journey of empowerment. "Tiffany, what change would you want to say as a business owner, looking at that whole empowerment piece, what needs to change?"

TIFFANY:

I would say this remains true. The workplace has been in existence for years, making sure you don't get stuck, that you pull in the right level of support, whether that's an HR consultant, the business coach, whatever that looks like. But it can't remain that way. A lot of businesses are so used to doing things a certain way. They have to be agile and they're starting to see that their policies they have in place maybe aren't serving them the way that they used to. Or that their teams want different things, and they need more for their development. The change is to be flexible enough to move into the future and offer flexibility. If you're telling people they need to come into the office five days a week, you're not allowing for that family time, that's a problem.

To be able to sync up to the true workplace needs is the change of the future. It's how we're doing it. It's really where businesses are going to be impacted. They're going to get the most productivity out of their teams. They are going to have engaged teams who feel like they're a part of it. And that's the other piece: allowing employees to be a part of the success and allowing employees to own some of that and help shape some of the policies, to have a voice in what that future workplace looks like.

SAM:

Bringing in outside perspectives is huge. And I think I'm seeing more of a trend there. Again, whether that's an HR consultant or a coach or someone else, it's important to see beyond kind of your own borders, your own doors, and see what else can be possible. You have to have your mind open to those possibilities.

Tiffany and I went on to discuss the negativity and trauma around the change in some of the large organisations, and the impact that this will have on tens of thousands of people's lives. On the flip side, we are seeing the emergence of great and fast-growing networks that empower one another, giving them the ability to work alongside some of these behemoths, which would never have been able to happen on the scale we are seeing today pre-2020.

TIFFANY:

I think a lot of people have trauma from corporate America and from some of their jobs at larger places. I think some of that feedback is fair, and we have to own that as business owners and leaders. But it is also a sweeping statement and a limiting belief. It doesn't open the door. There is collaboration in these smaller networks. I've been empowered to grow my own business through other people. And that crosses borders. Talk about doors being opened because we're working in ways that we haven't before. And yeah, you've had global organisations, but it's different now. And it's these smaller collectives who are coming together and using all their varying skill sets. When you look at the face of HR and how we're changing and growing and evolving, we have to pull in those other stakeholders to be able to help us shine.

I'm not a salesperson by trade. It's those networks that I've created and built that have empowered me. I've been able to thrive in my own business and then pour into my own clients and help them succeed too. It's pulling in the talents of the collective. You have to be this huge behemoth of an organization to have success. And what that really does, especially for women, is build your business tribe, as I call it.

And you build this collective of people who want to see you succeed and who you can pour into because where my strengths are, are someone's gaps. We can leverage each other's skill sets to really be empowered to lead in our individual organisations. These beautiful collaborations, like strategic alliance partnerships that we build, lead to things like the women's conference that I'm doing. We need to be able to say, "Here is a way to be impactful and to give people different voices." People need to hear different voices out there, not the same ones.

Diversity equity inclusion is here to stay. Then we look at how we're building teams, how we set them up for success in our organisations, or how we leave them behind. And that includes our leadership. They often get put from a technical role or into a leadership role without a whole lot of tools. That's not going to empower people. You need them empowered so that they can lead an empowered team.

Tiffany is a huge DEI advocate and has given many talks and appeared on numerous podcasts.

TIFFANY:

I think leadership and business owners should take a good hard look at their mission, vision, and values, and not just the one that are up on the website. Not just the diversity but the talent that they bring. That's been a gap that we are starting to close.

It's celebrating the team that you have and making sure that you're checking in on them. Having people understand that we need leaders to rise. It's about, what talent are you bringing in the door?

How are you engaging that talent? Just because you brought them in doesn't mean they're not going to leave if you're not embracing that. Make sure there's a budget set for diversity equity, equity inclusion. It doesn't have to be some big blown-out program. It's how you empower your people, how you're connecting with them. That connection piece is empowerment.

It's empowerment for leaders for the business and for their employees. You can start small. It's empowering to watch my small clients be able to start to build something that has become a model for other organisations who are even larger than they are. Think of the power of one organization doing that to become an organization that can be seen as a leader.

Tiffany finished by reflecting on her interview with me and a reader's takeaway.

I want [readers] to take away their own empowerment, their own belief in themselves to not have limiting beliefs in what they can achieve. We don't even know what we can achieve until we set out on this journey.

I've been so empowered in my own space, to be able to see what's possible, that I didn't even see coming. We manifest the blessings that we pour in. When you're starting out, it's so uncertain. Believe in yourself so fiercely that you have no choice but to manifest.

That, to me, has been just in holding onto my own values, in sometimes shutting out the noise and the comparisons of other people. You can go your own way and still be successful. You don't have to align with something that someone else is doing. And for me, that was a hard lesson, leaning into who I am and how I wanted my business to be versus, *oh, well, they're doing that over there.* I'm not doing that. Find your own measures of success.

5

Is It Really True?

*"A thought is harmless unless we believe it. It's not our thoughts,
but our attachment to our thoughts, that causes suffering.
Attaching to a thought means believing that it's true, without inquiring.
A belief is a thought that we've been attaching to, often for years."*
~Byron Katie

It sounds like such a simple question, doesn't it?

Ten years ago, I was receiving alternative therapy to try and help me fall pregnant. It was a desperate time for me as it was my final window of opportunity to grab that hallowed chance of motherhood.

The practise I went to several times a week had a fabulous therapist there who taught me many things.

The first one was that when we are born, we have a body and a soul. She drew two circles parallel to one another to represent each entity. She then drew another circle in the middle and explained that when we start to develop, so does our mind, and it begins to take over our soul and our body. If we are not careful, it can rule us and cause all sorts of problems.

She explained that if we can develop as human beings to be able to metaphorically remove our mind from ourselves and look at the thoughts that it is feeding us, then we have some semblance of control.

Let me bring this to life for you. I visualise my brain/mind as a British bulldog with wings, sitting in the passenger seat of a Mini. Don't ask how that thought came about. I literally have no idea. It works for me. Find an image that works for you.

I mentioned that the therapist taught me many things. I will also be eternally grateful for her introducing me to the work of Byron Katie, specifically, from her book *Loving What Is: Four Questions That Can Change Your Life.*

In the introduction, which is written by Stephen Mitchell, he talks about 'The Work' and the profound effect it has had on people from all walks of life. I would highly recommend everyone to read this book—and therefore, I will only share the first two questions with you.

1. Is it true?

2. Can you absolutely know that it's true?

Now take a step back from those questions for a minute. Think about a feeling or a situation where you've started the sentence: "I feel…" Or "They made me feel…"

Is it true?

Back during those days at Goldman Sachs, when I was getting yelled at for just breathing that day in the wrong way, and I felt the fear rising from the pit of my stomach, I would try and detach myself from that moment, focus on my breathing, and process how I would respond. I am sure that if I had read Byron Katie's book then, I would have coped much better outside of work, where I burned the candle at both ends as a coping mechanism.

Today, her book is one of my most priceless possessions. It's been written in, read, reread, dog-eared, and carried with me to many places around the world. It always will be.

I hope that it has the same wonderful impact on you.

6

Listen

*"Most of the successful people I've known are
the ones who do more listening than talking."*
~Bernard M. Baruch

There's a coaster on my desk with a beautiful photo of a sailboat on the water as the sun is setting with the words "Samantha—definition—good listener."

It's taken me years and many courses to truly listen; it's a skill that needs to be honed, refined, and worked on in business.

Without great listening and good questioning skills, we can so easily miss the next big opportunity. Time and time again, we are surrounded by people who listen to respond. Or worse still, can't wait for you to finish and simply start talking over you.

There's a great exercise that I get my group coaching clients to do. I split everyone up into pairs and ask one of them to tell the listener about a situation where they had a difficult conversation or one that didn't end well. Whilst telling the story, the listener isn't allowed to interrupt, ask questions, or show any signs of how they feel about the story.

Once the storyteller has finished, then the listener needs to respond and explain an opposing view to help create insight on the situation.

For example: during one of my courses, two founders had come together for the listening exercise. The narrator talked about a recent argument that had occurred between herself and a guest at a networking event. It was shortly after one of the lockdowns when masks were still required. She was exceptionally hot, and, as a menopausal woman, was suffering from the effects of having a mask on her face during a particularly bad hot flush.

She pulled the mask away from her face momentarily to try and slow down her heart rate and control her breathing.

A gentleman had walked by, observing her removing her mark, he remarked that she should really keep it on. She was irritated from the hot flush which was compounded by the bystander's comments and she snapped at him.

She explained what had just happened and, sadly, a short row ensued, which led her to suggest the two didn't circumnavigate in the same space for the rest of the networking event.

When she had finished narrating her story, the listener paused and reflected for a moment. "Perhaps they had a family member who was ill?"

I was party to this pair during the exercise. It had real impact; we'll never know why the gentlemen reacted the way he did. I can certainly sympathise with the narrator of the story during this exercise as I have been in a similar situation and have panicked many times when I've had my mask on for that very reason.

The power of this exercise is incredible; it shows us just how little we truly listen. Stay present, stay in that moment. Listen to what someone says to you, and more importantly, listen to what's not being said.

That's an art and one that's well worth mastering. In fact, listening earned me a deal worth £750,000.

EXERCISE

Listening is an understated skill, but it is a learnable skill.

Here's an exercise to test your listening skills.

It will take about 20 minutes. You can do this with a colleague, friend, or family member.

Your objective is to listen to the story that your partner is narrating without interrupting them or asking questions.

1. Your partner will narrate the story they want to share with you.

2. Listen to the whole story.

3. Now summarise what you've heard.

What did you learn through this activity?

What more did you hear by consciously listening to the story?

How does this differ from what you would normally do?

7

Judgement

"The most valuable thing you can make is a mistake—
you can't learn anything from being perfect."
~Adam Osborne

As I write this section of my book, I am hurtling towards London on a train. Many landscapes of my past are flying past me at breakneck speed. Good memories and bad ones.

How we judge others is also a reflection of how we see ourselves and our own limitations. It highlights our many complicated filters. It impacts our decision-making processes. In many instances, there might not be a right or wrong, and yet our judgement and everyday biases can tell us otherwise.

I grew up in an era and a society that thought marrying someone from a similar background was critical. Even as a little girl, that felt wrong, just WRONG to me. Surely values are more important? And there you have it—that's MY judgement.

53

But how does judgement affect our decision making, and what do we need to think about when using our judgement? First and foremost, recognise that we all have biases, and that's okay; the recognition piece is important.

There are a couple of ways to use your judgement when making big decisions.

For visual people, mind maps can be a wonderful way to think things through. Put the decision topic right in the centre circle and start to add satellite circles such as:

- What happens if it goes wrong?
- What happens if I don't do it?
- How will I benefit?
- What are my ultimate goals?
- Is there relevant legislation? (if that's applicable)
- What expertise do I need that I don't have?
- What lessons from my past do I need to consider here?

With judgement comes emotion, and the mind can play horrendous tricks on our judgement processing. In fact, this all comes from what neuroscientists describe as pattern recognition, which is a complex process integrating information across numerous areas of our brains.

I've talked about filters previously. These filters create judgement and influence our choices about how we are going to react and make our decisions. Because of this, pattern recognition can lead us to making the wrong decisions.

Brigadier General Matthew Broderick, Chief of the Homeland Security Operations Centre, responsible for alerting President Bush and other senior officials about the imminent threat of Hurricane Katrina breaching the levees in New Orleans, went home on Monday August 29, 2005 after reporting that the levees seemed to be holding strong, although there had been multiple reports of breaches. But how did he make that decision?

Broderick had previously been involved in operations centres in military operations, including Vietnam. He had previous experience of working in hurricanes whilst at Homeland Security Operations Centre. He used his previous experiences as they had taught him to wait and not rely on early reports as they can be false. Sadly, he had no prior experience with a hurricane hitting a city such as New Orleans, which is known for being a city built below sea level.

What happens whilst we are in these situations, making judgements? Something called "emotional tagging" takes place. This is when our emotions, also known as emotional information, attach themselves to our thoughts and experiences.

Our minds are wonderfully complex, so much so that each and every experience in our lives is stored across our network of memories. Just like pattern recognition, our emotional tagging helps us to reach sensible decisions—most of the time.

There are many examples beyond this. Think Blockbuster vs. Netflix, or BlackBerry, who dominated the mobile phone industry right up until the mid-2010s, vs. Apple. In the UK, BlackBerry dominated, enjoying a 33.2% smartphone market share in December 2011, according to Statista. Gartner reported in February 2017, just 210,000 devices with its operating system sold in the fourth quarter of 2016. It failed, and sadly, it failed spectacularly because it ignored the competition, such as iPhone, and rigidly stuck to its operating system—despite its significant flaws.

Judgement can cause major issues, but it can also bring about great opportunity.

8

Imposter Syndrome

"The beauty of the impostor syndrome is you
vacillate between extreme egomania and
a complete feeling of "I'm a fraud!
Oh God, they're on to me! I'm a fraud!"
So you just try to ride the egomania when it comes and enjoy it,
and then slide through the idea of fraud."
~ Tina Fey

Over the years, I have looked across meeting room tables and thought, "How have I got here?" Or felt that I needed to keep quiet as I didn't belong there.

It's a bit like being stuck in a sea of traffic with cars all around you and thinking, "Why am I the only one who ever gets stuck in traffic?"

Do you see where I'm going with this? Imposter syndrome is something that we ALL suffer from. However, it's how we deal with it that's important.

It can affect us in many different ways, physically and mentally. Labelling us with imposter syndrome is equally as challenging.

"In February 2021, we offered one simple idea: <u>Stop telling women they have imposter syndrome</u>. Since then, fixing the places where women work instead of fixing women at work has become a rallying cry for women of all races across the world." (Harvard Business Review article "End Imposter Syndrome in Your Workplace").

Life also has a cruel way of affecting how we see ourselves and making us question our own abilities. Whilst I was annoyingly positive about my life ahead of me at age sixteen, and I appreciate that I was in a fortunate position, my headmistress' comment to my father that I would "never amount to much" stung—and it hurt.

After I got over myself, I questioned why she thought that about me. Was it the fact I chose to go a different route academically and that I chose to be different? Or was it that she simply didn't believe in me, based on her entire career in academia?

Whatever is the case, comments that like, especially from early on in our lives, add fuel to the fire during those times where we feel imposter syndrome.

There's an element to it that can be healthy. Now hear me out on this before you read that again and shake your head in sheer disbelief that a coach would say such a thing. I coach founders to be comfortable with living in the uncomfortable. To grow as individuals, to help their teams to grow, and to change their relationship with failure.

The latter is a biggie. More on that in a moment.

Therefore, by constantly living in the uncomfortable—you are always going to be faced with challenges and situations where you feel you 'don't belong,' where 'I might get found out,' or you're not sure if you are 'good enough.' Feeling too comfortable in some of these situations can be equally as bad.

Arianna Huffington once famously said, "My mother taught me that fearlessness isn't the absence of fear, but the mastery of it. I leaned into that fear by trying to get into the Cambridge Union (the debating society,) where I eventually became the first foreign president."

I am by no means belittling imposter syndrome. When it takes hold, it can have devastating effects: anxiety and symptoms of depression that can result in a lack of confidence.

One of my long-standing clients has successfully launched a podcast channel, and it's attracting guests from the USA and the UK on some really interesting topics. The podcast hosts are introverted by nature and have been able to capitalise on their deliberate and calm manner. However, in a recent conversation, they said they felt nervous about the success of the podcast as they 'weren't like everyone else,' and that they were 'too quiet and just not interesting enough for it to work.' They were physically uncomfortable having this conversation, they couldn't make eye contact with me, I could tell they were embarrassed as their colour flashed crimson, and I could see they were sweating.

As their coach, I felt like I had failed them. We'd been working on their confidence in other areas, and I'd seen them flourish. All I could think of was the old adage "Just be yourself because everyone else is taken." They are now one of the most prolific networkers amongst my clients, which is a far cry from a couple years ago when they would do anything to avoid a crowded room full of eager fellow networkers ready to pounce on them. Plus, their business has grown over the last two years to needing an extra two people, and they are currently in the midst of a recruitment drive.

The podcast is the latest in a line of activities they have had to lean into when their subconscious was strongly recommending they walk away. We are now recording the third series. They are much more confident and, in fact, recently said, "I'm actually enjoying it now."

Sometimes, imposter syndrome is easier to overcome than other times. If you are reading this and really connecting with it, I hope this helps you recognize the pain, face it bravely, and overcome it.

"I don't know whether other authors feel it, but I think quite a lot do—
that I'm pretending to be something that I'm not,
because even nowadays, I do not quite feel as though I am an author."
~Agatha Christie.

Interlude

Interview With Jen Coken

Sam:

If you could put yourself back in your shoes when you first started out, what's the best piece of advice you'd give yourself today that you'd give others?

Jen:

I don't know that it would be one piece of advice, but the first that comes to mind is: be willing to try things. We get caught up in trying it the "right way" or finding the person who's going to tell us what the strategy is or what the path is, and we'll follow that and we'll be successful.

It's no accident that that kind of thing happens because so many out there go, "If you do it this way, you can make lots of money." Well, know this: *your way is unique to you*. There may be some basics in there, but we have all eventually found our way and our unique message and our unique clientele.

61

In other words, investigate, try things on. If it's not working for you, don't do it. Try something else on. And if somebody says to you, "You really should," with that certainty like some of those gurus do, stop and check in with yourself to see what resonates with you.

Someone suggested something to me last week, but I knew that's not the way I want to do business. So always check in with yourself. If you need somebody to help you check in with yourself because you're not on such sure footing, have some thought partners to ask to talk it through with you.

Sometimes what happens is the people we talk things through with are agreeing with us rather than acting in the role of mentor and listening and asking questions to get us to think things through. Sometimes I'm a verbal processor. I need some thought partners. So don't be afraid to make mistakes, try things, and don't take everything people say as the truth. Check it out for yourself.

Sam:

There's real power, isn't there, in those thought partners. How do you go about identifying your thought partners?

Jen:

Well, for me being a part of the Dames is one of the ways. I feel like you're one of those thought partners. We can go back and forth. "And what about this? And what about that?" I think it's just like any good date. It's partially chemistry, right? You have to go on a few dates. You have to meet a few people and see if you jive, jive, jive. Clearly words are escaping me today. Good thing I'm doing a podcast right after this.

You don't have to make a connection if it isn't there. I had one thought partner from the Dames, but our calls are on hiatus now. From the beginning, we would spend an hour a month together. And she was really going through a reimagining of her business and was moving away from an entire business she had built and searching for something new.

I was really able to contribute to her, just helping her work through imposter syndrome. She's also a brilliant marketing person. She was able to read my marketing content or ask me questions. I think it's figuring out, first of all, what do you need in terms of a thought partner? Is it talking through your ideas? Is it a mastermind? What is it? And then trying some people out like a date and figuring out who that right fit is.

Sam:

When you look at, say, your journey as a business owner when things weren't going well, what was your biggest learning then?

Jen:

As a business owner, you have to understand there are ups and downs, and sometimes it's day to day. My most recent happened when I just started listening to too many opinions. It's too much, it's too much information. And I just had to sit in stillness with myself and check in to see what worked for me and my business. Because that was the moment where I wanted to fly to Bermuda and get lost in the Triangle. You have to recognize there are always going to be moments for growth. As you elevate, your business elevates, right?

This is what my content writer and I were just talking about. We've been working together for four years now. She's like, "I feel like we keep looking at the messaging because it hasn't ever quite sat right with you." It's never quite. And she wrote a blog post. Sam, I was in tears reading it. I'm like, "This is it. This is so it, this is what I've been trying to say for years. This is it. Yeah." So there's always growth.

What did you learn from it? It's coming at it with a beginner's mind, let's say, from a Buddhist perspective or a learner's mind. This is where success comes in. "I will succeed if I'm grossing $500,000 a year or a million dollars a year." You know what kind of life you're going to have, the personal lifestyle you're going to have. If you're grossing a million dollars a year, not much of one, unless it's the kind of widgets you can sell to hire a bunch of people. So do you really want that? Is that really what you're going by? What's freedom for you? What aligns with you? I think it's important what you said, which is coming at it with a learning mentality and a growth mentality.

Sam:

I like that. And it's funny, I've been reading lots of things recently. There seems to be a trend right now, where people are saying things like, "Run your own business and find your own freedom." What irritates me about that is running your own business does not give you freedom. It gives you the ability to be able to grow more as a person. You are no longer a slave to a monthly salary. And I love that analogy that I've heard recently. I no longer want to be a slave to that. The freedom comes from your growth.

Jen:

Yep.

Sam:

My husband said to me recently, "I don't think you do this for the money. You do this for the output. And having someone say to you, *oh my God, I've just done that deal that I never thought I could do, Sam.*" Or someone crying on the phone and it's awful, but something I say really hits them and it's gone. That's it. That's what I need to solve.

Jen:

Yep.

Sam:

The money is the output of what we do, which facilitates us to do this.

Jen:

You find the joy in fulfilling your purpose. You feel like you're fulfilling your purpose when you're doing the work that you're doing. When I'm doing the work I'm doing, I feel like I'm fulfilling my purpose, but I don't have more freedom. Oh, get more and open up your own company. Are you kidding me?

The first three to five years are the hardest. You must understand how to delegate. And you're now responsible for potentially employing other people. There's freedom in being able to pursue what you are passionate about versus being part of a machine that's fulfilling somebody else's vision or somebody else's brilliance or producing widgets.

Sam:

Yeah.

Jen:

None of us who do what we do in the service-based businesses do it for the money, really. I don't think.

Sam:

No.

Jen:

The money comes when we're in flow. We pursue our passions and the money follows.

Sam:

Absolutely right. And there's lots of fear in setting up a business, right? And this is exactly where you come in with all the good work you do. What one message do you want people to see down in black and white in this book that says "You got this." How's your way of helping them with that?

Jen:

I'd say two things. One, your fear isn't real. The body sensations are. The sweaty palms, the sweaty armpits, the feeling in the pit of your stomach. Those body sensations are real, but the brain is never actually dealing with reality. The brain's job is to keep the brain alive, which is you. So it's constantly determining whether you're going to survive whatever that thing is.

Only, we're not talking about getting eaten by a dinosaur. We're talking about opening up your own company, right? So that fear isn't real out there. What your brain is doing is predicting the worst possible outcomes so you can figure out a way to survive. If we can get a handle on that and start to witness our thoughts and practice non-reaction, practice just being an impartial judge and jury like, "Oh, look at that thought going by," just observe that thought. We have thoughts and opinions about everything, from the car we drive to someone walking down the street. You already, in your head, know if they're a nice person or not a nice person.

We think our thoughts actually control things. They don't. Have you ever said, "I really hope it doesn't rain tomorrow." But you're there in Britain. It probably does rain because it's Great Britain and there's a lot of rain. Your brain can't control things.

For me, it's reminding people the fear isn't real. You're completely capable. You're unique. You're brilliant. Can you be an impartial witness to those thoughts and just notice them floating on by rather than reacting to them? Because it is our reaction where the suffering comes in. The meaning we add to it, the reaction, the thinking our thoughts are real, and they're not.

Sam:

I love that. I love that. And is there anything else that you think would be helpful to add when you are looking at the three pillars of empower, create, and succeed?

Jen:

I think number one, whatever business you want to start, there's some business plan out there for it already. Use that as your steppingstone. You don't need to reinvent the wheel.

I think what's key, and it's a step that a lot of people miss, is creating your vision that you imagine for the world. And your vision is the way you want to see the world. My vision is a world of people at home with themselves. And then you're on a mission. You're on a mission in this lifetime to fulfill that. My mission is to empower women executives and C-suite level leaders to own their brilliance, to own the masterpiece that's inside.

Make sure you take the time to create the vision, to create a visualization board, to do that kind of a thing, and then find the plan. There are lots of resources out there. Then test and retest, test and retest, and find allies along the way to help support you. Particularly those times when you don't believe in yourself, because sometimes other people believe in us far more than we believe in ourselves. It's true for everyone.

EXERCISE—SELF-AUDIT

Think about a time where something at work or in your personal life has not gone to plan in your eyes.

1) How did you get in your own way?

2) What are the common fears or barriers that you recognise you have at those times?

3) What does your mind tell you during these times?

4) Write down five words that label how you have felt from the work you have done in questions 1-3.

5) Write down five empowering words that connect with you.

6) Put the five empowering words up in view of your workstation.

WHY FAILURE IS A LEARNING CURVE

Remember, the most successful person in any room has made lots of mistakes and has felt just like you.

1) What did you learn from what went wrong?

2) What will you do differently next time?

3) What are you most proud of through that situation?

4) How do you feel about it now that you've looked at it as a learning exercise?

Now that you've completed both those exercises, what new skills are you excited to learn?

9

The Rule Book of Today

"Success is not final; failure is not fatal:
it is the courage to continue that counts."
~Winston Churchill

There is no rulebook—that went out the window in March 2020, as far as I'm concerned. Why do I say that? You know why. I remember how it initially felt like we were all back in some wartime effort, except we couldn't see the enemy.

It felt like we were all one big community, good old Blighty! As the weather warmed up and the days seemed longer, we all stood on our doorsteps each Thursday night to clap the NHS heroes, wine, beer, or G&T in hand, raise a glass with our neighbours. Barriers were broken down between neighbour and neighbour.

We had the time to get to know one another. We cared as we all went out for our ten thousand steps a day.

Friday, 8 May 2020, marked the 75th anniversary of VE Day, and again, people celebrated this extra Bank Holiday with picnics, barbeques, and bunting in abundance. The weather was glorious and the mood was still upbeat.

People's personal lives seemed to have slowed down. After all, the two-hour expensive and tiresome daily commute was no more. However, jobs were being lost and people were worried about the future may hold.

Others had that 'light bulb moment' of wondering why they had invested so much time and money going out to an office each and every day, when in actual fact, they could roll out of bed at 06:59 and be at their desks at 07:05. Slight exaggeration, but you can see where I am going with this.

According to The Average, Microsoft Teams grew to 145 million users in April 2021, up from 115 million daily users in October 2020. Zoom said it had 300 million daily active participants in 2020, and relative platforms such as Slack revealed it had 12.5 million "concurrent users."

I decided to launch MindAbility and was met with surprise and ridicule. Did I not see what was going on in the world? How many more coaches did we need?

I stood firm. I felt it in my heart and soul that if now wasn't the time to share my experience, to build a community, to help a community, and find new ways of working, then when was?

What I have witnessed and learned since then has been phenomenal. I've experienced a rate of growth that I have never seen before. Amongst my community, I have witnessed exceptional mindsets as well as heart-breaking stories.

LinkedIn rapidly became a place that supported me as I built my community. I'd moved back to an area I knew from my childhood. I felt lonely and isolated as I'd left my friends in a completely different part of the country. The shutdown didn't help, but LinkedIn has been a platform that I will be forever grateful for.

Small business owners weren't waiting for someone to come along and tell them what to do or how to navigate such turbulent times. They grabbed the opportunity with both hands and saw that new networks, sectors, and technologies were needed. Those already in certain spaces quietly acknowledged that accelerated change and advancement in technology wasn't going to slow down. Far from it, the door had been firmly opened and they'd sprinted out into the new era.

What made these people different? Mindset, grit, resilience—all words that we see and hear around us the whole time. People like me playing with them as if they are everyday skills. They are for some. Let me give some examples of what I mean.

Cinemas were replaced by streaming services. Netflix became our friend, and a good one at that. How often did you hear people talking about 'binge-watching' and those team calls where the first couple of minutes were spent exchanging recommendations?

Lovemoney.com wrote an article in February 2022 which read, "Data from movie industry website The Numbers suggests that significantly fewer people are now venturing out to the cinema, with annualised figures claiming just 511 million tickets could be sold this year, down from over a billion in 2019.

"By contrast, the demand for streaming services is skyrocketing. A study from Grand View Research has shown that the video streaming sector will experience a compound annual growth rate (CAGR) of 21%, meaning it will hit a market value of $223.98 billion (£164bn) by 2028."

Those late nights, plus the increased and acute competition, are not for the fainthearted, and I have seen many consultants go back into full-time work. The flip side of that is that those who have consciously chosen to write their own rule book, build their own network, and put the grind in are now succeeding.

10

The Hindrance of Comparison

"Believe me, comparison sucks the creativity and joy right out of life."
~Brené Brown

The grown-up term for this is social comparison theory, which was developed by psychologist Leon Festinger in 1954. According to *Psychology Today*, "Social comparison theory is the idea that individuals determine their own social and personal worth based on how they stack up against others."

I compared myself to others for years—not thin enough, too fair (I'm that one that looks like I've lived in a cellar for the past twenty years when I get into a swimming pool.) Why didn't I think like XYZ? Why is my tummy so fat? I could go on and I know many of you reading this are nodding your heads thinking, "Yup, that sounds just like me."

The Good

There are elements of comparison that are aspirational. We want to emulate the habits and motivation of people who we perceive as being more advanced than we are in specific areas.

How we react to comparison is the crucial part of all of this. Creating the right habits to bring about the change we are looking for takes discipline, focus, and a recognition of who we are. That means our capabilities, our potential capabilities, and our aptitude.

Beware of the Traps

Theodore Roosevelt's famous quote resonates when he called comparison "the thief of joy."

Whilst comparing ourselves to others can be empowering and uplifting, it can also put unnecessary pressure on us and lead to us feeling unworthy and incapable.

For business owners, particularly those in their early stages, I see this all too often, sadly. "Why can't I be more like XYZ?" or "I'm not going to do as well because I am not as outgoing as XYZ." It can lead to resentment, poor decision making, and burnout.

Coincidentally, I was on a call last night with my coaching cohort. I had two very different ladies on the call. One was towards the end of her career and had set up her own HR and L&D (learning and development) consultancy to fit in around her lifestyle.

Her mortgage has been paid off. She's got two grown-up children who she proudly told us earned way more than her now and have two good holidays a year. She explained that she doesn't want to grow a large business. She's not interested in working long hours again. She's been there and done that for many years in the corporate world. She's got a handful of clients on retainer, and she's looking to keep that.

The second lady was in a very different stage of her life. She has three young children, she's a single mum, and is a wellbeing coach. She wants to build her business, write a book, build a digital platform to support her consultancy business, and she only wants to work 3.5 days a week. She's ambitious with purpose and is adamant about how much she works in the week. She's working ridiculous hours that she fits in around the children. For example, she told me she regularly starts some of her work around her book and building content for her digital platform at 9 pm at night and frequently finds herself still working at 1 am. (I know, I know, and she's a wellbeing coach, we did have a conversation on that point.)

The two are incomparable, and yet, I had to remind them both of that as there was a slight and unspoken awkwardness once they'd both outlined what they were looking to achieve. Why is that?

The subconscious automatically gets us to compare. Put simply, we are ALL individuals, we all have our different filters and different perspectives, and we are all *whole* human beings first and foremost with our own minds, ambitions, hopes, and fears.

I hope that makes sense, because by recognising who WE are and by appreciating our many attributes whilst recognising what we're not good at, we can identify when and how comparison can be an aspirational emotion and avoid that which will only cause us harm.

11

Failure

*"I can't give you a sure-fire formula for success,
but I can give you a formula for failure:
try to please everybody all the time."*
~Herbert Bayard Swope

Even that word can cause people stress, right? I used to put myself in that camp. After all, I'm on my third marriage (sounds awful when I put that down in writing.)

However, there is a power behind it. If I hadn't had a failed online retail business, I wouldn't have the conviction or insight around my core strengths or building B2B businesses, specifically those in the HR and people consultancy space.

I wouldn't have the business I have today. I most certainly wouldn't be writing this book. All this thought-processing has helped me change my relationship with failure. I truly hope in this section of the book, I can help those that are afraid of failure to take that leap and accept that. Sometimes, it's just not going to go your way, and that's okay. It's how you deal with it that matters more than anything.

When I was a little girl, I had the most disastrous morning. It was the type of morning that happens once in a blue moon, even now as a forty-something woman.

It was a Saturday, and to help my mum, I decided I would feed the dogs and generally help her. I was only nine at the time. We had two gorgeous beagles who loved warmed oats (porridge) in the morning. I took their bowls (aluminium), made their breakfasts, and we heated up their morning meal lightly in the microwave as it was cold outside and they were partial to a warm breakfast.

Anyway, I put said dog bowl in the microwave with the breakfast, thinking I'd cut out the middle bit and save on the washing up of an additional glass bowl. I felt very smug about the whole thing and hoped I could show my mum that she didn't need to heat up the dog's food in a glass bowl and then transfer it.

I turned the timer on the microwave for twenty seconds and, well, it looked like an electrical light show going off in the microwave. As I marvelled at this lightshow and wondered why I had never seen the microwave do this before, my mum walked in. Needless to say, she was absolutely FURIOUS—livid, in fact. She made me open the microwave after explaining the error of my ways and why you should never, EVER put a metal bowl in the microwave.

Feeling thoroughly chastised, I decided I'd go outside and see my dad. I KNEW I could help him around the garden. Besides, it was probably best to leave my mum to give her some time to calm down and appreciate that I was simply trying to help and not blow up the kitchen.

Dad had a small lawnmower he said I could operate to help him. *Marvellous*, I thought. *Time to lend a helping hand.* Within five minutes of being helpful, there was a very loud crunching noise. I'd accidentally mown over a large jagged stone, which damaged the blades.

A ditzy young girl? Maybe. Probably. Okay, definitely. But I remember how the failures of that morning and the reactions of both my parents (my dad was also far from impressed with me) totally ruined my weekend. I sulked about the place for the rest of the weekend and felt completely misunderstood and couldn't wait to get back to school on Monday, which for me was rare as I wasn't a fan of school.

Whilst this might not be business related, there are many comparisons here. I was trying to do what I thought was the right thing. One thing after another simply went wrong, and the feedback I got was right, but it was tough to hear.

We have that in our working lives too. We are all going to make mistakes; frankly, it's how we learn. It's *how* we learn to deal with it that makes a difference.

So what happens now when I make a mistake? Like I said, I deal with it. But if that 'failure' or 'bad judgement' can be seen as a learning moment, then it can alleviate the stress of it all, whilst helping me to see how not to do it again.

As I'm sure you can imagine, there have been plenty of studies around failure. We've all read about and watched many YouTube videos and podcasts around how the release of testosterone and dopamine affects our brains. Over our lifetimes and via our experiences, when we 'win' at something, our brain comes to see it as a habit. Many biologists call this the Winner Effect.

Yup, you've got it. If there's a Winner Effect, there's got to be something that's the opposite of that. There's always conflicting research on topics such as this. What saddens me is that some research suggests that failure can impede our concentration and it's that which sabotages our performance. When I think about it, if I'm on a diet, I know that I shouldn't be having those fries, but do I still want them? Hell yes! Do I give in and fail? From time to time, of course.

What's my point? It's that it's okay and, if I don't make a regular habit of it, I'm not going to beat myself up about it.

So if you are going to fail, fail fast. Learn from it and write down why something went wrong, what will you change next time. Recognise how you feel after you've reviewed and addressed the situation.

EXERCISE

On a scale of 1-10, where were you at the beginning of this section when you thought about failure? One is being in fear of it and ten being you are comfortable with failure. Where are you now with it?

What can you take away from this section and keep with you as you grow your business?

12

Managing Stress

*"Stress is a balancing act. Too much = burnout. Too little = boredom.
In the middle is where you find your superpowers."*
~Allison Graham

Well gosh, if I had the cure, I would be a millionaire. In fact, I'd probably be a billionaire! From time to time, stress can get the better of us and sabotage logical thinking or physical and mental health.

I used to hear friends and colleagues in offices say "I don't have time to be ill" as they dragged themselves into the office because they felt obliged to do so. I'm no exception to that rule. Putting ourselves second doesn't help anybody in the long run. You know the old adage "Put your own oxygen mask on first." There's a reason for that. If we don't look after ourselves first and foremost, we can't look after and support others in the long term.

During my mid-thirties, I had a spell when each winter I would come down with something nasty: kidney infection, labyrinthitis (which is like a vertigo), influenza, shingles, etc. Yet, I would worry about my work—constantly. That element of self-induced pressure has held me back. It's only now, looking back, that I have realised how many challenges I put in my own way.

In August 2021, a Betterup.com article on managing stress in the workplace said, "The American Institute of Stress found that 75% of employees believe they have more on-the-job stress than a generation ago. While 1 in 4 employees view their job as the number one stressor in their lives."

Is this self-induced? Is this reality? Were the previous generation just stronger than us?

I've walked away from writing this section of the book for two straight days. My book coach calls me a 'steady writer,' but this bit has stumped me. After three days of walking, exercise, getting a good night's sleep, eating particularly well (and by that, I mean really healthy foods), I realised why. I was putting pressure on myself, re-searching and rereading books and articles that I have stored up over many, many years.

I have just demonstrated and lived my point. So much of the stress we put on ourselves today is self-induced. Don't get me wrong, I am fully aware of the struggles that so many of us are going through.

So why is it then? Maybe it's because machines are doing so much for us today that we are naturally less active in a more natural and sustained way. To demonstrate my point, a few generations ago, we would do our washing by hand, scrub it, rub it, put it through a mangle, which took energy and kept us fit. What do we do today? We shove it in a washing machine and then, if we don't want to or can't put it on a washing line, we throw our wet washing in another machine to dry it.

It's extreme, but when I thought about it and really stepped away, science, articles, books, they are all great, really, they are. But we are all more stagnant today. Hell, I'm one of them. I can quite easily work for sixteen hours each day for five or six days straight and have only three hours of exercise over that same period of time. That's not good—that all adds to our stress levels.

We talk about digital detoxes and again, there's something in that. We are surrounded by our laptops, phones, iPads, multiple TVs, and a 24/7 connectivity to the outside world, in whatever version we choose to follow.

All these machines in our households impact how we sleep. In my home, we've invested in a 'blue shield' that counteracts all the waves given off by these devices, helping us to detox and sleep.

In recent times, we've gone totally organic, decreased our portion sizes, reduced our intake of junk food (but gosh it's so good), and upped our intake of vegetables with every meal. It's amazing the difference it's made. We sleep better, our quality of sleep has improved, and I can most certainly get through a hell of a lot more each day.

My one takeaway on managing stress is it's a series of little things that are right for you, your family, and your lifestyle that will have impact. Most importantly of all, and my biggest learning from this small section is: don't overthink it. Lesson learned.

13

Turning Sorrow to Light

"That's because you is both criminals."
~Anonymous Police Office

After my partner died many years ago, the deep, deep trauma of it all was incredible. Literally, one moment I had a normal life, building a life with him, building a home, both working hard to pay off our mortgage, and working hard to create our long-term home. Then one day, it all ended abruptly. He died suddenly. My life became a whirlwind of autopsies, police statements, arranging funerals with his family.

During that time, we had to go and identify his body. We all went, my parents and his family. The police came and picked us up, and the officers were incredibly kind. They worked with us as if we were the only family grieving. Sadly, the sole purpose of these wonderful human beings was to work with families just like us.

I wanted to sit at the front of the police car on the day we had to identify his body. I needed to get my own thoughts together before

91

what I was about to face. On the journey there, and as the gentle hills rolled past us, I began to smile. Drivers passing us couldn't work out what two elderly looking women and a relatively young blonde were doing in a police car. Funny what our minds do to protect us during these times. They can sabotage us during normal times, whilst protecting us during our deepest, darkest hours.

When we pulled up at the morgue, silence fell, the false cheer left, and the sheer rawness of it weighed heavily in the air. I got out of the car, and as I closed the door, I heard 'the mums,' who were in the back of the car, complain that they couldn't get out of the car and that something was wrong.

The officer, without any hesitation and with a gentle smile, turned to them both and said, "That's because you is both criminals" with an ironic policeman's accent that he put on for effect. Both the mums roared with laughter. His kindness and gentle humour at just the right time made the following half hour so much more bearable. Kindness comes in many forms. This extreme example taught me a lot in a very dark hour of my life.

As I write this in the Spring of 2022, it feels like many people around me are dealing with sorrow, disease, potential poverty, and many, many other world issues. But here's the thing: during these times, it's how we fight for our ourselves, for our families, and for our beliefs that's important. Sometimes, not all the above are conducive with one another, far from it. I've heard and experienced families who don't work together, who have lost their way under the principal guise of "sticking together and family first."

Why is this so important? There will be times in your business where it feels like no one believes in you, where things are so tough that you have dug as deep as you feel you can go. There IS always light at the end of every tunnel. We CAN and WILL turn sorrow into a great shining light. I've learnt this firsthand in running businesses. That's okay, I promise you, we've all been there. What's the best thing you can do at such times?

Look after YOU. YOU are the most important and most valuable asset in your business. Find your tribe, find those people who are aligned with you, what you are trying to achieve, and where you are heading.

Find those people who have built their businesses and have faced the challenges that you are facing, and talk to them. Talking to people and being open to change is critical. You WILL get there, you WILL succeed—it just might be in a different way than you had originally thought.

14

It's Okay Not to Be Okay

"It's okay that I got sick, I suddenly realize.
If Lyme hadn't taken me down so radically,
I wouldn't have learned about stillness.
I would not have discovered my enormous capacity to endure.
I would not have embraced this deeply contemplative place within
my own being."
~Katina Makris

How often do you look at social media and think, "How do they do it?" or "I wish I could be like them" and beat yourself up about it. Stop! Please stop! It can lead to you feel unsure about where you are at, what you are doing, and about succeeding.

Having said that, we can't have all good days, in spite of what social media tells us.

Those days are okay, truly they are. Those are the days where it's best to switch off. Be kind to yourself, and if you need to go on a long walk and leave your phone behind, then do just that. You will feel so much better having taken the time to deal with it.

I get some of my casual wear from a great and ethical brand called Om & Ah. With each order, they include a postcard. I kept one of them and it sits on my desk. In fact, I take it everywhere I go as it means so much to me, although it's looking pretty dog-eared after having it for a few years now.

It reads "The goal is to grow so strong on the inside that nothing on the outside can affect your inner wellness without your conscious permission." It's attributed to HOMEBODY CLUB. I've got to admit that I don't know anything about HOMEBDOY CLUB. The thing is, there is so much truth in this—and I consider it part of my evolution and journey of self-discovery.

I've built my own resilience reserves and recognise that there is only so much I can cope with as a human being and all the complications of an active, ambitious mind.

There will always be knockbacks. It's how we cope with them that defines us. I talked about finding light in sorrow in the previous section. That has helped define me, but I had to sit with and deal with a lot.

Sometimes it's hard to get back up again and carry on. It's during these moments that I don't feel okay. Yes, I'll have a good cry on occasion. My go-to when I'm not feeling okay is to find water—a local lake, a river, the sea—anywhere that I can breathe through it and process what I am going through. Bottling it up only means I need to deal with it later. Surely that's not healthy.

How often in our lives, when we are feeling this way, have we heard "Just smile, the world will feel like a better place" or "Sending sunshine your way" from very well-meaning friends who aren't sure how to best help us?

We've learnt that this is known as 'toxic positivity'—meaning that it doesn't matter how bad we are feeling, we should still maintain a positive mindset. Frankly, it belittles and invalidates how we are feeling at that time.

Explore those feelings at the time you are having them and deal with them at the time you are having them. The worst thing you can do is bury your emotions. We are complicated human beings, so recognising that and looking after you is critical.

Running our businesses is no mean feat, and very few people appreciate what it takes until they've tried it themselves.

15

Resilience

'The future depends on what you do today."
~Mahatma Gandhi

Resilience: the capacity to recover quickly from difficulties, toughness

Yes—we are onto resilience! At the end of this section, I'll share with you a handy exercise that will help you to build and maintain your resilience.

Firstly, what is it? It's a word that's thrown around – *a lot*. Well, many people think it's the equivalent of running a marathon, on one leg, blindfolded.

Resilience coaching is a much-needed and booming industry. It gets 36,600,000 results in Google UK for a wide array of personal coaching, wellbeing coaching, and executive coaching. It all sounds great, but as a budding business owner, how can you go about building your resilience?

Good question. Firstly, resilience is something that starts at home. We are living in a world full of seismic changes and massive challenges that we never thought we'd see in our lifetimes, and our roles and relationships are evolving, sometimes in a way that we never thought. That can be perplexing, inspirational, or even hurtful in some instances.

Being able to feel comfortable with the idea of living in the uncomfortable is how I describe developing our resilience. It's a state of mind that's not always easy to maintain.

WE need to change and adapt our habits, our perspectives on how we live our lives, and how that impacts our world of work, particularly if we are business owners facing a rising tide of rising costs, inflation, and wars. Leo Tolstoy wrote, "Everyone thinks of changing the world, but no one thinks of changing himself."

So true. How often have you heard people say "Great to see things going back to how they used to be." That statement ignites mixed emotions for me. Firstly, frustration. We will never go back to how it was. What we've been through is all part of our evolution. However, we can control elements in our lives, especially as business owners, and THAT'S the exciting part—the part where resilience comes into play.

Those of us who have understood there is no rule book any longer, that we can build communities around the world of

100

like-minded, value-driven business owners, who also have different opinions and perspectives, can only help us to evolve.

That evolution is all part of building our resilience. By learning fast, adapting, and working forward, we as business owners are learning that we can create our own narrative and futures.

One of the key elements to building your resilience is self-awareness. Truly understanding your aptitudes and how you want those to evolve is the key. Remember, there's real power in the statement "I don't know how to do that… yet."

Reframing adversity and understanding the FACTS, separating those, taking learnings, and where possible the positives out of those situations is of critical importance.

I remember my turning point. Adversity was all around me. I was dealing with the raw emotions of losing someone I loved, someone with whom I thought I would spend the rest of my life. The legalities of the whole thing after he died, in terms of an unknown world ahead of me, very nearly broke me.

Each night, my wonderful friends in California would call me and we'd talk until I fell asleep. They came over to stay with me and helped me. They talked about their raw emotions and their sense of loss. My goodness, that was one of the times in my life where I showed up in my pure, devastated, and desolate state.

It was during this period I returned to work and went on my infamous 'walk.' I was told that my fellow shareholders were concerned about my performance. This was twelve weeks into losing my partner.

This individual, who was with me on the walk that day, meant me no harm and had gotten it wrong—that was not the case at all. Yes, my fellow shareholders were worried, but they were more concerned about my state of mind at the time and how they could support me.

Can you imagine hearing that when you feel that all around you is crumbling? The violent end of one life and the brutality of the next that is still slapping you in the face each day.

That one comment made me stop in my tracks. I felt the most powerful emotion well up from the very bottom of my soul—it was an energy I had never felt before. I felt released, released from caring what others thought of me, and focused on what I could do for others.

That one moment has led me to where I am today. It has defined me, made me stronger than at any other time in my life, and I draw off that emotion—resilience—each day.

It's led to my intense journey of self-discovery. They say it's never too late to learn, and that is very much the case for me. I devour more books than I have ever read before. I've studied gender diversity, neuroscience, and learnt about other peoples' journeys and proactively try to understand their 'why' in the deepest sense of the word.

Resilience. It's a massive subject. There is a plethora of fabulous books out there that can continue to help you. In short, it's being comfortable living in the uncomfortable. It's about learning, adapting, and leaning forward into your life.

EXERCISE

Taken from: https://positivepsychology.com/resilience-activities-exercises/

Take Your Resiliency Inventory

The late Al Siebert, PhD founded The Resiliency Center in Portland, Oregon. He developed a quick resilience test.

Take this quiz, adapted from The Resilience Advantage (2015).

Rate yourself from 1 to 5 (1 = strongly disagree; 5 = strongly agree):

- I'm usually optimistic. I see difficulties as temporary and expect to overcome them.

- Feelings of anger, loss and discouragement don't last long.

- I can tolerate high levels of ambiguity and uncertainty about situations.

- I adapt quickly to new developments. I'm curious. I ask questions.

- I'm playful. I find the humour in rough situations and can laugh at myself.

- I learn valuable lessons from my experiences and from the experiences of others.

- I'm good at solving problems. I'm good at making things work well.

- I'm strong and durable. I hold up well during tough times.

- I've converted misfortune into good luck and found benefits in bad experiences.

Convert your scores with the following key:

Less than 20: Low Resilience — You may have trouble handling pressure or setbacks and may feel deeply hurt by any criticism. When things don't go well, you may feel helpless and without hope. Consider seeking some professional counsel or support in developing your resiliency skills. Connect with others who share your developmental goals.

10-30: Some Resilience — You have some valuable pro-resiliency skills, but also plenty of room for improvement. Strive to strengthen the characteristics you already have and to cultivate the characteristics you lack. You may also wish to seek some outside coaching or support.

30-35: Adequate Resilience — You are a self-motivated learner who recovers well from most challenges. Learning more about resilience, and consciously building your resiliency skills, will empower you to find more joy in life, even in the face of adversity.

35-45: Highly Resilient — You bounce back well from life's setbacks and can thrive even under pressure. You could be of service to others who are trying to cope better with adversity.

16

Power of Self-Talk

"Your self-talk is the channel of behavior change."
~Gino Norris

Turn "I Can" into "I Will"

How many of you talk to yourselves? It's normal, we all do it, and it's a really powerful habit.

When we are facing adversity, many of us will say to ourselves, "You've got this, Sam" or "I CAN do this" when we are faced with something that is way outside our comfort zone.

There are many neuroscience experts who describe self-talk as a remodelling of certain situations. As part of remodelling, people use their own name, just as I did above, when referring to themselves. Experts say this is because we have more acute feelings of self-confidence. Whilst those who have less confidence will say "I've got this" when using self-talk.

Using your name during self-talk also gives us healthy perspective as it allows us to step back and look at the situation we are faced with that's causing us to self-talk in the first place. It can alleviate stress levels as it gives us fresh perspectives.

However, we also need to be mindful of negative self-talk as this can hold us back.

I recently heard a client (different to the client I was talking about earlier who also has a podcast) say they didn't think their podcast was as successful as others because they were quieter than a lot of the other podcasters they admired. They didn't think they could sustain or grow an audience base as people may find them boring because of their quiet and more measured approach.

I wanted to get to the heart of this statement. I wanted to create that insight where they could change and control their own narrative outside of our coaching sessions. Franky, it broke my heart to see this strong and self-assured business owner feeling this way.

Outside of our sessions, they constantly put off doing any work towards getting guests on the podcast, although the first series had been a huge success at gaining subscribers. Because of a regular flow of content and the great conversations, they even won a couple of new clients out of it.

Their perception of themselves as being inadequate happened *because* they were making comparisons. It was limiting their enjoyment and opportunities.

We had several discussions around the power of quality conversations that had come about in the first series of the podcast. I wanted them to see that people who may have a quieter disposition are often seen as deeper experts: people listen, really listen to them.

I asked questions around some of the talks they had given recently. What feedback had they received? They replied that they were invited back to give further talks, and invited to write articles and thought leadership pieces for this publication. That's because their talk and the quality of the content was so well received.

And finally, the penny dropped. It was okay to be quiet. In fact, their approach was working for them. Their self-talk changed after that session to "Scott, you're going to doing this your way from now on."

We are now pre-recording series five as I write this book. The podcast is being picked up by a growing audience in the UK and USA, and people are regularly approaching my client to ask if they can appear on the show. They've even been approached by a sponsor!

There's a lot of research out there about the power of labelling our negative feelings. It helps us to deal with them far better as we can gain more control over them because we've labelled them. Identifying feelings helps us deal with them.

So the next time you hear yourself using negative self-talk, label that self-talk. Ask yourself questions as to why you are feeling the way you do. Then look at the times where you have done things well and have been able to celebrate those successes. Apply that to the current topic you are challenging yourself with. Now do you see how you can turn that negative self-talk into something much, much better and learn to overcome it?

17

Record Your Celebrations

"Celebrate your success and find humor in your failures.
Don't take yourself so seriously.
Loosen up and everyone around you will loosen up.
Have fun and always show enthusiasm.
When all else fails, put on a costume and sing a silly song."
~Sam Walton

You've won that big client you've been working on for months. You've nailed that new skill you didn't think you could master six months ago. How are you going to celebrate those wins?

It's important to take the time to celebrate these wins as it helps you to relate to them when self-doubt creeps in or you are facing a rocky patch for whatever reason.

It's spring right now, and as the sun comes up, I love nothing more than to be outside, wrapped up against the cool morning air as the sun rises and shares her energy with the world.

As I go on these walks, I pass fields of miniature hors-es and idyllic English countryside cottages adorned by mossy thatched rooves and dancing daffodils exploding around their wooden fences.

I consider this walk, which I do two or three times a week, a celebration. I've got my health. I've got my friends and family. I've got a thriving business with dreams and ambition to turn into something even bigger than it is today.

Fast forward sixteen hours later when I'm still sitting at my desk at night, tired and dry-eyed from being in front of the screen for so long, I look back at that small celebration of the morning and it keeps me going.

Thank goodness I went on that walk—*that* is my small celebration. It doesn't have to be big. In fact, sometimes something as basic as an early morning walk can help you to celebrate.

My belief is that we need to see the growth of our businesses as a series of campaigns, simple stages of growth. It means we can plan for a beginning, a middle, and an end. We can work through each campaign, monitor our progress and results, or change things up where we need to if things aren't working as we'd hoped.

We have a clear result that we are looking to achieve and end date. By hitting that, it's time for my clients and their teams to celebrate. Some have given their teams a couple of hours off on a Friday afternoon, a bonus for a particularly large project that went well, gifts, or verbal recognition where it's deserved.

Celebrating our wins is critical, truly it is—it will help you to keep going; it will get you through the bad times and help you get to where you want to be. There's a big difference between getting where you need to be and where you want to be. Celebrating is a key element to getting you to where you *want to* be.

EXERCISE

1. List your last three campaigns.

2. What did you achieve?

3. How are you going to celebrate the end of the campaign, your wins, and all you've learned from them?

4. How are you going to implement what you've learnt into future campaigns?

18

Learn Something New Every Day

"Any fool can know. The point is to understand."
~Albert Einstein

Eighteen months ago, I was giving a keynote talk to one of London's largest employers. They'd asked me along to give a talk about resilience and to share aspects of our work that could help their workforce who were struggling with the many aspects of remote working and being on lockdown.

It was getting towards the end of my talk, and I was taking questions as we went along. This session was theirs. I didn't want to be one of those passive speakers that just talks at people. I wanted them to ask questions, share their perspectives, and collaborate.

Click, next slide—"Learn Something New Every Day." That was the title of my slide. By creating new habits, learning new fun facts, reading a bit of a book, maybe even working towards learning a new skill, we can continue to evolve. It's also a great way to manage stress, particularly for those who feel incredibly uncomfortable with dealing with change.

It was incredible! Suddenly, the chat filled up, people had learnt to cook new cuisines, learnt to knit, learnt new health and fitness habits, taken courses in their own time, and learnt new languages (Mandarin, Spanish, Italian, and even Latin). One person wanted to do all the things that they were scared of. Next on their list was a skydive! Braver soul than me, I can tell you.

They were learning new things about one another. There was a lot of "Oh wow, that's amazing" and "Love to chat about that. Maybe that's something I can get into too," and the most obvious one, "I never knew you did that."

My talk that day had a two-fold benefit: my audience saw the power of learning something new each day and grasped my point about self-evolution. They also saw their colleagues in a different light by learning something new about them.

Those that were more introverted used the chat box to exchange ideas and feedback. Those who were more extroverted shared hilarious tales of attempting to cook a complicated dish and how they managed to create the equivalent of a London fog in their kitchen in a matter of minutes, knitting escapades that were a complete disaster, open water swimming clubs, and new friendships blossoming as a result with people that they would have otherwise never met.

Learning something new each day is also incredibly reward-ing. I know that building a business is all-consuming. I'm writing this on a sunny Saturday afternoon whilst everyone else is in the garden, and that's okay. I had my walk at sunrise.

I read every day, I listen to podcasts, I've subscribed to many newsletters to help me learn something new every day. I took up knitting again after twenty years last winter and have knitted blankets and scarves. Most of all, I know I have evolved. As my business grows, it helps me to continue to evolve. To be open to change, different views, and perspec-tives, and to challenge my own, to always challenge my own.

So what new thing are you going to learn today? What will it be tomorrow and the day after that? These are important questions for you to explore.

EXERCISE

1. List seven things you want to learn over the next week.

2. Record what you've gained from these activities.

3. How has it helped with your self-development?

4. What has it given you?

19

Blurred Lines

"The privilege of a lifetime is to become who you truly are."
~Carl Gustav Jung

We turn up to work as our entire selves, when previously, we showed the world what we *wanted* them to see, in many instances hiding our authenticity. Our value lies in our authenticity.

By turning up as our entire selves, we are changing the dynamics of the way we work. We are changing where and how we set personal boundaries between work and home.

Lately, I have been talking about menopause and my journey with it on LinkedIn. I've talked very openly about my challenge with hair loss and the impact that it's had on me and my confidence. Many women have reached out to me and shared their stories of the menopause journey. It's been heart-warming and tragic to hear their tales and to witness their willingness to open up on this deeply personal subject.

Authenticity is one thing; however, we still need to have clear boundaries between our work and personal lives. This is becoming increasingly difficult in a world where so many of our businesses are either hybrid or 100% remote.

But where and how do you set those boundaries? The first one may sound so obvious: identify what the boundaries are that you want to set for you and your team. Is it around defining flexible work hours, dress codes, team interaction? Only you know where you want to set those boundaries. Identify those boundaries, why they are important, and what it means to the business. Communicate those boundaries to your team.

For those of you who work with consultants and outsourced teams, share with them as well because they are still representing your business. Explain to them why these boundaries are so important to you and the business. Ask for their feedback. This helps everyone honour the boundaries and stick to them.

For example: some companies have introduced a policy where their teams rotate to finishing early on a Friday once a month. It's a great way to thank the team for their hard work and dedication. It is also a wonderful employee engagement incentive. Whilst the sun shines, half the team gets to leave at 2 pm on a Friday once a month, and the other half two weeks later within that month.

This has come about as many of the team members found it hard to differentiate between home and work after they'd moved to

100% remote working. People were regularly sending messages late into the night or over the weekend and their CEO would challenge them to stop working. She was really concerned about the blurred lines she was seeing. She had a dedicated and committed workforce and she wanted to protect them.

Each day, the lead manager would send a message to those she could still see online after 6 pm, wishing them a good night and asking what they were still working on. We came up with a mini campaign—'say goodnight and mean it.' Meaning, when the last of the team was still online, we wanted to know what they were working on and identify if it really had to be done that night. Invariably, it didn't and when we wished that team member goodnight, we wanted them to log off and enjoy their personal time.

The campaign lasted about three to four months, and we worked with the lead manager and team to ensure that they weren't working for working's sake. The Friday afternoon incentive has also helped encourage them to explore new things that they can do outside of work and is a great talent attraction and retention tool.

This is just one example of how setting boundaries has had a positive impact.

For some employees, they want a physical boundary of an office and a home, due to their personal circumstances. Some of my clients have had staff members who lived in a one-bedroom flat. Their employees' bed has become their sofa, office space, and bed. It's simply not healthy and it's completely understandable why they want to go to an office each day.

The rise of community offices and shared workspaces offers small business owners the opportunity to have an office and provide that social connectivity for their employees who need to get out of the house and work elsewhere.

Creating a work routine is critical to success. For example: I walk two to three times a week, and I have my PT session at a set time twice a week. I write my to-do list each Sunday for the following week, and I update it at the end of every workday in a specific notebook. I've had the same type of notebook for the last five years as I've discovered the routine that works for me.

All my conversations and notes I take down in my digital notebook. Each client, partner, and supplier has their own section in my digital notebook. Each conversation is marked by date so I can easily refer to it when I need to.

I've created two desks and office spaces at home: one where I do my heavy thinking and a small studio for my podcasts and PR related work when I'm onscreen. These are my boundaries that I've set for myself.

Decluttering is also an important part of being able to function well as a business owner and maintain focus. Harvard Business

Review wrote a great article on how less clutter will help to decrease levels of stress and anxiety whilst increasing productivity and focus.

Boundaries are all about self-discipline, great communication, and habits. I think of them as a contract, a contract between myself, my team, and my clients. It helps maintain healthy relationships, which, in turn, reduces stress and unnecessary conflict. After all, haven't we got enough of that in the world already?

Part 2:

Create

20

Goals – Be Specific

"All successful people men and women are big dreamers.
They imagine what their future could be, ideal in every respect,
and then they work every day toward their distant vision, that
goal, or purpose."
~Brian Tracy

It doesn't matter what size business you have. The more specific you can be in your goal setting, the better. Remember those goals you had when you were working in a big corporation, or for someone else, those SMART goals? Well, they are going to come in handy now.

Just to recap the old mantra:

- Specific (simple, sensible, significant).

- Measurable (meaningful, motivating).

- Achievable (agreed, attainable).

- Relevant (reasonable, realistic, and resourced, results-based).

- Time-bound (time-based, time-limited, time/cost-limited, timely, time-sensitive).

The bad example that we see all over the internet is the one that states, "A bad goal is when you say you want to get fit this year."

A SMART goal would be: "I want to build up my fitness this year to be able to run twelve miles in eight months' time. I am going to run three times a week, one of which will be with a local running club, to achieve my goal."

There are thousands, probably tens of thousands, of groups across social media that encourage people to hit $10K months. "When was your first $10K month?"

The bottom line is that if you haven't got your pricing figured out, your VALUE, who you are selling to, and that emotional connection with your prospects, that $10K is going to be hard to hit for a lot of people.

Specificity is the name of the game. Be careful not to fall into the trap of confusing an objective with a goal. **Goals** have a dual purpose to help set long-term and short-term objectives, which can be broken down into individual points. **Objectives** are the milestones that you want to achieve under each goal.

Let me give you an example: if your goal is to have ten new clients in six months' time, then part of your objectives could be to attend three events over the next three months to acquire said clients.

There are other aspects to consider when you are creating your goals. Who else will be responsible for supporting you in achieving these goals? What objectives do you need to set to reach those goals? How will you track and monitor the progress of your goals?

Lead by example and communicate well. By that, I don't mean communicate more often. I mean communicate well. That can be difficult in a virtual office and is reliant on you building trust with your team and understanding what they want to get out of a role within your organisation. The beauty of today's world is that working with our teams is more of a joint effort, or relationship, than we have seen in previous eras. Personally, I think that's a great part of our new workforce of today.

Goal setting is not easy. It requires you to have good data and the ability to be able to set clear goals. They are an organic tool within your business and shouldn't sit on a drive somewhere gathering dust once you've built them. Far from it. Review them weekly, monthly, quarterly. Are these goals still relevant? How do you need to change them, if at all? What roles need to change or be added in the team to help you achieve your goals? Was the data you used right in the first place? (More on the last question in the next section.)

If this isn't your forte, I strongly advise you to find yourself a mentor or a coach. They could be the difference between you spending a lot of time and money in having to readdress this further down the line.

Let's take a step back and work out how and what to measure. This will also help you refer back to this part of the book at a later date when you are looking at goal-setting.

EXERCISE

Goal-setting can be tricky, largely because we don't go into our goals in enough detail to bring them to life and make them happen.

Here's a simple exercise to help you set some realistic goals and to get you thinking.

Write your thoughts down on a separate piece of paper and keep coming back to it and adding or editing over the next couple of weeks. Live with it for a bit and see how this goal develops for you.

BIG PICTURE: What is the outcome you are looking to achieve?

(This goal could be focused on home or work.) For example, you would like to purchase a farm in five years' time, 80 acres, or a new car in two years' time.

What do you need to do to achieve this goal?

For example: generate $xx more revenue each year, change jobs, introduce a new product or service, expand your business by xx%.

What needs to change?

Evaluate:

Is your mindset holding you back?

Do you need a coach to help boost your knowledge and confidence?

Do you need to introduce new habits?

Where are you now?

Write down where you are on this journey at present.

What milestones would you like to set along the way?

How will you measure these milestones?

How will you celebrate them?

What obstacles might you face?

How can you overcome them?

Are there any new skills you might need to develop or buy into your business to achieve your goals?

If you do need new skills, when will you need them (e.g.: end of year 1, mid-year 2)? It's totally fine to add this as an estimate.

My final question to you is:

How often are you going to review your goals to see where you are and what needs to be changed or updated?

Goals WILL change. That's okay. The most important thing is to keep them alive and let them be your motivator.

A Final Word

How and where you put your goals is a personal thing.

Some people build vision boards and put pictures of the house they want to buy, or how they want their life to be. Others simply have a photo on their desktop.

Put your goals somewhere that you can look at them regularly as a reminder of what you are trying to achieve and what you need to do to get there.

21

To Measure or Not to Measure, That Is the Question

"When the student is ready the teacher will appear.
When the student is truly ready... The teacher will Disappear."
~Tao Te Ching

"I've been really busy lately."

"Great" is my standard response every time I hear someone say this to me, particularly when I hear it from a prospect. Why is that?

Largely because I want to know if they have been busy with sales, or more importantly, doing the *right* things for their business to grow and succeed.

When you are first starting out in your journey as a business owner, entrepreneur, or whatever you choose to call yourself, it's a frantic time. You are the brand strategist, the marketer, the salesperson, administration, and in some cases, the accountant too.

Once you know who your ideal client is (and I do mean *who*) and you've identified where they hang out and that emotional connection you can build with them, it's time to work out your sales and marketing (obvs). When we start working with clients, we have a focused questionnaire that asks a series of questions, many of which they are unable to answer, and that's okay, truly, it's okay.

Here are a few things that you really DO need to measure to help you scale your business in the right way and have control of that growth.

- Social media content – how often you post (if you haven't done so, think about getting an automated content scheduler. There are some great ones out there. Canva has a nifty one, Hootsuite has one, check around.)

- Number of cold calls/DMS – track this daily or weekly.

- Number of leads – again, track this daily or weekly.

- Source of those leads – track this and track it well.

- How many contracts you've sent out in any given week.

- Renewals (great for account management purposes).

This is all great as it shows you the impact that the above activities will have. Some will obviously work better for you, depending on which service or product you promote.

The other tool that will be invaluable to you is a factored sales pipeline. This will help you to see what's coming in and from where and will become part of your dashboard.

What is a factored sales pipeline? Let me give you an example: if you have a prospect in your pipeline with whom you have been in talks, would you 'factor' them at 25%? That is having had an initial conversation. Or would you give them a factored value of 50%? That could be 'proposal sent.'

Is that making sense? The total sale value is NOT what's in the pipeline when it comes to a factored sales pipeline.

We love 'em. If you are looking for more of an understanding on this, reach out to us. We'll share more about this with you.

22

Power of Focus

"You only have control over three things in your life – the thoughts you think,
the images you visualize and the actions you take."
~Jack Canfield

I'm what's known as a parallel thinker—which means I often have several thoughts going on at the same time. It can be maddening in that I always need to work on staying present with what I am doing, who I am talking to, and even writing this. I'm thinking about my next coaching session with a client later today. *Stop it Sam, just stop it!*

All right, all right, you are wanting to read more about the power of focus, tips on how to focus, and the obvious one: the juicy benefits.

The power of focus, in most instances, is logical. For example, I was recently working with a client who explained that they calculated they spent 60% of their time networking, and as a result, they only had 7% of all their sales from their efforts.

As part of their homework one week, I asked them to go away and calculate the time they were spending on all their outbound and sales activities and the results from these.

They took a lot of the data from the factored sales pipeline we talked about in the previous chapter.

It was a real 'ah-ha' moment for them. All that time and money for such small return. That focus enabled us to look at several things: were they going to the right networking meetings? Was the message right, were the usual business networking meetings the right way, or were there other more profitable routes to market?

How do you form the habit of focus? Firstly, and the most obvious, is consistency. Consistency in your marketing and content creation on platforms like LinkedIn and Instagram. That consistency will please the algorithms and help to raise your profile to your perfect prospects. I appreciate that business, life, and all manner of other things might get in your way. That's understandable. However, the greater your consistency, the greater your results will be.

There will come a time when you simply don't have time for certain things that you have tried to create the time to do on a consistent basis. That's when it's time to outsource those activities.

Secondly, work on one thing at a time. Once again, it's one of those things that sounds so obvious, doesn't it? Believe me, when things start getting busier for you, it's so easy to tackle several small tasks at once, and before you know it, your morning or afternoon has gone and you feel like you haven't achieved what you wanted to.

Block out time for the bigger activities and make sure that time is not open for negotiation. It's easy to make excuses and put things in during this time, but please don't. Starting and finishing your projects in one hit can conserve your overall time. Maximising your time will become a critical skill that you really need to master—and fast.

Block out time for your social media too. That can be such a huge distraction the more you get into it. I have had many clients who have lost two hours a day simply scrolling. Trust me, I've done it too. A great coach of mine made me block out one hour a day for social media. That was the best habit I have created and has helped us build a thriving business today as a result. It's made me do the *right* things.

Finally, and as demonstrated by my client at the beginning of this chapter, stay focused on where you are placing your energies and measuring the results you get from them.

We can all be busy, but let's help you to be busy doing the right things that will help your business to grow and provide the life that you want it to. After all, you are building a business on your terms to give you freedom—however you define that freedom.

23

Power of Coaching

*"Your comfort zone is a place where you keep yourself
in a self-illusion and nothing can grow there,
but your potentiality can grow only when you
can think and grow out of that zone."*
~Rashedur Ryan Rahman

Oh, how I've looked forward to writing this chapter! My first piece of advice to you is find a coach that you can relate to, someone that feels like your pragmatic champion. I'd recommend that one of your first questions is to ask them if they have their own coach. My alarm bells always go off if a coach doesn't invest in themselves. How can they expect you to invest in them if they don't practice what they preach?

As you can tell, it makes my blood boil when I hear of that. Also, find a coach with experience, not one that follows a process to the letter as they've only built up one business, or worse still, have been an employee and then decided to be a business coach.

Coaching can be so powerful and can help in many ways. Most of the time, a great coach can create insight for you, share their expertise, and push you out of your comfort zone in a psychologically safe environment that they have created for you.

Along my journey, I've invested in LinkedIn coaches, and I've invested heavily in my own business coach, someone who is ahead of me and is living the lifestyle and running the business that we are striving to have. My vision is to be an international business coach that is recognised as helping founders to succeed and grow their business on their terms for the benefit of their friends and family.

I'm delighted that we have achieved that using a blend of my existing traits of tenacity, relentlessness, open-mindedness, damn hard work, and taking risks.

I've got a long way to go, but I want to learn each day. I want to grow every day. I am open to learning new viewpoints and perspectives; in fact, I welcome conversations with people who have different ideas and beliefs from me. How else can I learn?

Even writing this book, I have a fabulous book coach. I feel accountable to her. She keeps me going. She has given me such great advice and support when writing this book. She helps me see my progress, which motivates me to keep going, and answers questions as they arise. I have wisely invested in what I am doing and it's paying off.

From here, I will also invest in a coach to help me thrive in my keynote speaking career. I'm not afraid of the camera or public speaking; in fact, get me in front of an audience and I love it! Always have. However, there are certain skills that I recognise I don't have.

I regularly get feedback from clients that I have asked them the uncomfortable questions they haven't been able to address themselves. I work hard to create that psychologically safe place for them before I go there.

A client recently described me as a "pragmatic champion" in a testimonial. "What's a pragmatic champion?" I asked. I was flattered when they explained that it was because I never told them what they wanted to hear or appeased them, far from it. I helped them to see the root of challenges, which was sometimes painful and always resulted in us fixing them. I'll take that—in fact, I will frequently use #pragmaticchampion in my hashtags.

Coaching will help you to grow as a person and a business. It will challenge, support, inspire, and empower you. It will help you to achieve things you wouldn't have thought possible, and you will meet the most amazing people.

Many business owners want to spend their money elsewhere, and sadly, end up losing a lot of money because they've been doing the wrong things.

In the US, coaching is a part of everyday commercial life. In the UK, we are still lagging and don't value it as much as I believe we should. What a shame. Let's change that.

24

Pragmatic Champion

"The world is full of magic things,
patiently waiting for our senses to grow sharper."
~W.B. Yeats

Being a pragmatic champion, in fact being labelled as one, has really helped me to define my persona—and what makes it even better is that it came from a client. Who could ask for more, really?

What's my point? Think about *who* you want to be and how you want to be perceived. Do you want to be the next Brene Brown of the coaching world? The next Daniel Priestley of the business coaching world?

Take your time to really think about it. You will be amazed at how this will help you to describe yourself, describe and define who you want to work with, and to visualise where you want to get to.

Embrace it, use it with good humour, and across all your content. You'll see that you start to create a voice, one that sounds authentically like you.

It's so easy to go into that vanilla language when talking to a room full of fellow networkers or across social media and to sounds just like everyone else.

You need to be brave. There will be times when people don't like your opinions, and that's okay. We can't all agree with one another. By defining who you are, you will always be your authentic self, and believe me, it will be far easier to tackle those negative comments on social media if and when they happen.

25

The Power of Habits

*"We are what we repeatedly do. Excellence, then, is not an act,
but a habit."*
~Will Durant

There have been many books and articles written about the power of habits, some more memorable than others.

Habits aren't created overnight. We grow up brushing our teeth morning and night, then we learn a new habit of having a cup of coffee or tea in the morning. We develop a habit of having a smoothie in the morning before our PT explains that that's a bad habit and we need solid food first thing to break the fast. So now we need to create a new habit.

You get the point? Just because you want to post on social media each day doesn't mean that you will create the habit to do so. That requires discipline on your part, largely because a habit comes from a region of our brains that is hard to control.

Our brains operate on a cue-operate-reward feedback loop, which was discovered by those clever people at MIT in 1999. Charles Duhigg later called this 'the habit loop' in his book *The Power of Habit* (a great book, by the way, if you haven't read it).

The habit loop is broken down into four parts: Cue, Craving, Response, Reward.

Cue is all about the trigger: the time of day you expect to do something (such as your morning coffee), a certain location, an emotional state, maybe a smell, a person, or a sound.

Craving is self-explanatory as it's about what causes that craving and how our brain anticipates the reward, which is what motivates you.

Response is the engagement piece of the habit and the action you to take to get your desired outcome.

Reward, again self-explanatory. This is about the outcome and how you are going to satisfy that craving—the pleasure aspect, if you will. It's this part of the loop that creates the craving for the next time you carry out the habit—and so it goes on.

For example: let's say that each Friday you reward yourself with a glass of wine, a pint, something that is your end of week celebration. Others might go for a walk, meet friends for dinner, go to a movie. Whatever it is, the brain is programmed to crave that each week.

Let's say you want to break that Friday habit of having alcohol. That's going to take effort because it's a *habit*. First and foremost, reflect on why that habit is bad for or why you want to change it.

As a result of changing that habit, it may help you achieve your goal of losing weight. Stay present with the habit in the first few weeks. It will be tough, and there may well be times where you want to hit the 'bugger it' button.

Things to help break or create a habit include journaling, if this is something that's helpful to you, or finding an accountability partner. They are great when you are trying to create new habits or break old ones. You know that weekly call is coming, and it is a real incentive.

Our brains are complicated machines, huge networks for data and experiences that will always remain in our networks. New habits are formed and overlayed over old ones and that's why the power of habits is just that—powerful!

Here are some habits to create that will put you in good stead to build your business:

- Spend an hour each day on your social media to build authentic relationships.

- Create your sales pipeline dashboard to have on your desktop and update it daily.

- Create a spreadsheet that tracks how many posts you do daily/weekly, cold calls, proposals, and contracts you send out, renewals, etc.

- Find regular self-care activities to help you maintain your wellbeing. I personally take quiet walks. My book coach swims. Whatever uplifts your energy, do it.

26

Get Comfortable Being Uncomfortable

*"Be willing to be uncomfortable. Be comfortable being uncomfortable.
It may get tough, but it's a small price to pay for living a dream."*
~Peter McWilliams

Running your business is never going to feel comfortable. Period. There will always be firsts—first big win, first big client loss, first employee, first office—I could go on.

As part of that evolution, you will constantly change and evolve alongside your business.

Some of my clients have come out of corporate after a couple of decades of service at a senior role. They have been so used to running other people's businesses that no one has taught them how to run their own. They can quickly run into problems.

The art of selling is an area that many small business owners struggle to contend with, particularly those who are in the B2B space.

Many founders fall into the age-old trap of selling time for money. There are only so many hours in the day, and, at the beginning, probably only one of you. So what happens when you fill that time up and you want to sell something else?

Being uncomfortable is a good thing—it means you are constantly growing. If you grow, then it helps you to help your clients to grow, adapt, and achieve their goals.

Some of my clients have shunned trying new things such as podcasts or public speaking because they are concerned about failure. It's more about the unknown. The emotion of doing the tasks that make us feel uncomfortable can signal a reaction in our brain not to do it. The thing is—just do it. Yes, you will feel uncomfortable, and yes, you will also feel so much better for having done it.

In writing this section, I found over fifty-two million results on Google, all telling us to do things like go for walks in the cold wearing shorts, or to take an ice-cold shower once a week to get us comfortable with being uncomfortable.

Personally, I'm not a fan of that kind of stuff. I *am* a fan of pushing ourselves in our day-to-day lives, particularly as business owners. It's taken me a long time to come to grips with elements of social media—the technology and tools required for Instagram, the fear of putting myself out there on LinkedIn.

What's happened because of my giving it a try? Well I've learnt to let go and turn up as me, just me, each and every day on LinkedIn and have built up a great business as a result.

I've got all sorts of apps on my phone to help me make reels on my Instagram. I'm not saying they are perfect, nor am I going to make any excuses for them. I'm learning, I'm evolving, and I'm putting myself out there, even on the days when I don't want to. I'm learning to embrace being uncomfortable every day, and frankly, I'm loving it!

EXERCISE

When was the last time you did something that was completely outside of your comfort zone?

What did you learn?

How will you take that learning to do something different today, tomorrow, or the next day?

27

Thinking in the Most Unusual Places

"The mind is not a vessel to be filled, but a fire to be kindled."
~Plutarch

Where do you do your best thinking? First thing in the morning when you're out walking the dogs? In the bath or shower? Or most frustrating of all, that 3 am lightbulb moment that has you up, wide awake. You've planned world domination, and then, bugger it! You've forgotten what it was in the morning when you wake up at your normal time.

Bizarrely, it's the distraction of what we are doing outside of work that helps us to come up with our brilliant ideas. When our minds aren't thinking about work-related matters, our alpha waves ripple through our brains, with a specific spotlight toward remote associations within our brains, coming from the right hemisphere.

We can sit at our desks all day long, trying to fathom out a challenge or come up with a creative idea for our next campaign. We can spend our time solving problems analytically and carrying out our work, but it never works as well as those lightbulb moments. What I'm talking about is those inspirational, super creative, right brain moments.

Shelley H. Carson, Harvard psychologist and author of *Your Creative Brain*, explained that little distractions such as bathroom breaks, getting up and stretching your legs, etc., can be a good thing when it comes to creativity.

Some of the biggest ideas in history have come from sitting in the bathtub. Archimedes came up with the principles of density and buoyancy whilst watching how the water flowed whilst running his bath. His lightbulb moment came when he realised he could determine the density of water by submerging an object and working out how much water had been displaced.

Although my ideas were nowhere near as impactful as Archimedes, they weren't bad. I used to take the same five-mile walk each day during lockdown. At first, I came up with a flow of really good ideas. As time went on and those weeks turned into months, I was coming up with fewer and fewer ideas during my walks. Until there was nothing—it was simply a time for me to unwind and stop my brain from thinking.

Something was up. Surely this wasn't right. I changed my routes up every few days, and the funny thing is, my internal 'ideas factory' started producing again. It felt like I was having more focused ideas. They weren't so vague and they were better quality. Why? I suspect it was because I changed up my routine.

I've learnt to keep a notebook on my bedside table. I use a Remarkable as my digital notebook (other notebooks are available obvs); that always comes with me too, just in case. I just know that pesky idea is going to hit me during a dinner out with friends or slap bang in the middle of nowhere when I'm thinking of things other than work. The alpha waves are flowing and the dopamine is in abundance. Capitalise on it—that's where the magic happens.

28

Sell What *They* Want

"If you channel your time and energy into solving problems, money will channel itself into your wallet."
~ Utibe Samuel Mbom

It's all too easy to set up a sales meeting and prepare for what you want to sell without any thought for what the company you are meeting *actually wants*.

It's a common mistake. The problem is, both parties leave the meeting slightly frustrated; you've not got a sale and they feel they've wasted their time.

How do you avoid falling into that trap and how do you sell in a way that the customer or client wants to buy?

The most obvious one is that you are there to listen to them—*their* needs, *their* challenges, *their* aspirations. I know it's going to sound harsh, but they are probably not that interested in your son's graduation last weekend.

People buy from people, I get that. You know that annoying aunt/uncle friend who always dominates the conversation? What happens when they do that? Rarely will you take in what they are saying, in fact, far from it. Your mind wanders off into so many other directions—anything but the conversation at hand. That's what happens in meetings like this—it is all about *them*. Period.

Before and during the meeting, find out what they want to achieve. Ask them how you can best support them. Use your natural curiosity and be brave.

You might feel slightly awkward asking some of those tougher questions you really want to ask—and often, that's where you need to get to. Asked in the right way, they will land well and can be hugely insightful for everyone in the room.

Let's go back to selling what they want. When arranging a meeting with a prospect or an existing client, find out what they want to achieve by the end of the session. What does success look like for them? That in and of itself can be a powerful question.

It may only be a couple of small points that are different when putting together the agenda. Quick sidenote whilst we are on the subject of inviting a prospect to a meeting: if you find out that you are not meeting with the decision maker and you are as far away from a sale as an eskimo in the balmy Dubai climate, then is it worth going? Your time is valuable.

It's hard to go into more detail on this point—the essence of this is much more impactful, and always be mindful of it.

Now is a good time to look at some of your forthcoming meetings. Ask yourself: have you set a structured agenda? Can you send them a short bullet-pointed agenda and ask if there is anything they would like to change and/or add?

How has this made you feel about the meeting ahead in terms of your focus? Were there any differences between your agenda and theirs?

Interlude

Interview with Terry Bower and Gareth Dimelow
of Inside Stories

SAM:

Creating a business takes time, effort, and a hell of a lot of gumption. To create a great business, you need great people around you.

I've been incredibly fortunate to have found some wonderful folks, including the co-founders of Inside Stories, Terry and Gareth. They are business story strategists and help company owners to unlock their WHY, HOW, and WHAT by creating meaningful, memorable, and moving elevator pitches.

In fact, through their work, they've helped numerous companies secure funding who would have otherwise landed up in the ever growing 'no' pile for investment funding.

I wanted to know what advice they would give a business owner who was picking up this book and who needs inspiration.

GARETH:

"I think that business owner, or would-be business owners, anybody who is at the beginning of a journey rarely thinks about planning the journey they set off. And it's kind of a "I'll see what comes up as I go" because particularly if you're running a business, there are a bunch of practical considerations. You need people, you need product or a service. You need pricing, you need all those logistical fundamentals.

And I think the idea is that all the other stuff, which is just seen as peripheral, will present itself, fall into place, announce itself as something that needs to be addressed, and when, but the inception point of the business is, I need to start doing the thing that I do or that I know how to do or that I really want to do.

"And I'll speak to this many clients and I'll win this much business and I'll have this much turnover. There are other people who can help with that." And that's all valid. Our point is the story is putting in a framework, putting some guidance around where we are going as a business, so that every conversation that we have, every opportunity that we encounter, every challenge that we have to overcome is done with a sense of unified purpose so that there is some rhyme and reason rather than we're just batting away challenges as they arise. It gives us an aim, like a touchdown to come back to that reminds us that we

are doing the right thing that keeps our head in the game, that keeps

us focused on the right direction, because it's very easy to be distract-

ed by the other things.

Terry and Gareth run workshops with their clients, and there are always so many inspirational 'aha' moments. I wanted to know more
about the commonality of these moments.

GARETH:

"The commonality, I think for us is the moment where the client realizes

that they're being heard, because I think so many people in this space

reach a point where they consider themselves to be experts in their field.

They're marketing experts, communications experts. That's fine. I'm not

challenging that expertise, but it's very easy when you position yourself

as the expert to assume that you already know everything.

I think clients, particularly startups, would be business owners.

They're trying to figure out who they are, and if they haven't figured

it out yet, then there's no way some external body could have. "Yeah,

I've already got you. I've got your measure of you. I know where

you're going. I know what you're doing." You can only do that by

listening, and for us, Terry calls it the penny drop moment. It's the mo-

ment where they're suddenly hit with, "Oh my God, you didn't just ask me a question and then tell me what you thought the answer should be. You asked me a question and then you waited and you listened, and when you played back what you heard, you gave me a new perspective on a thing I've been struggling to articulate for the longest time." That's the lightbulb moment for me.

TERRY:

"That's every single client we work with, without question, and you can see it in their eyes. It's that moment where there's a change in their face, change in their persona. Their shoulders drop. They're just more relaxed. They're at ease because it's quite a stressful process actually at the start, especially if it's a single business owner.

I get to sit and be the devil's advocate. And I get to sit in almost on the client's side, which is great because it challenges Gareth every time. That's why the process works. The fact that they're being listened to, they can relax and say anything, is what works. And we have conversations that go off in whatever direction, but it always comes back to that point. I know that sounds a bit wonky, but it's an inner truth.

SAM:

I was curious to know how they saw the world of entrepreneurship shifting over the next few years, especially in light of the fact that many experts are saying that up to 60% of job titles we will see in the marketplace in 2030 aren't even here yet!

GARETH:

"Sam, you posted about this on LinkedIn, just yesterday, about how many businesses used the word "difference" but never bothered to who extrapolate what that difference is. And I think it's because, when you set up a business, it is intensely personal. It is so very different to having a job working for somebody else where you just assimilate into the wider organization. When it's your business, it's your skin in the game, it's your DNA at the heart of the business. And if you haven't done that introspective work, unlocking the person that you are and the thing that drives you as a human being, you will never have that connection to the business. Consequently, you will always struggle to explain it. Coming back to your question, looking to the future, the idea that the roles of tomorrow aren't even in existence yet, I think that's always been the case.

It's certainly been the case as long as we've all been alive. Every generation has a bunch of new roles that the previous generation had never heard of. It's one of the reasons that there'll always be some kind of generational divide between children and parents as they go out into a world of work that didn't exist for their parents. This is not a new phenomenon. It's as old as any of us can remember in our life-time. There's a comfort factor in that. There will always be new roles that don't make sense. Our opportunity is in working with clients to prevent them from being distracted by what's going on in the rest of the world. And it's not about being insular.

I use the word introspective specifically. It's about looking inward and asking, "Who and what am I, and what is it that I'm looking to achieve in the world?" Because then the changes that go on exter-nally have very little bearing on where I'm going and what I am, as long as I'm true to my own direction of travel, to the course that I've plotted for myself and my business. It will be that much easier for me to pivot, adjust, evolve, and adapt in accordance with those wider societal transformations and evolutions that take place because I'm following my North Star and everything else is just like the weather that you pass through.

SAM:

I love that. Follow your North Star. Brilliant. My last question to you both is what surprised you about running your own business? What's the one piece of advice you'd give based on what you know today?

GARETH:

Terry touched on the things I was mulling over when you asked the question. I think it would be trust in your value rather than worrying about your cost. Because what we do costs a certain amount of money. Some people who maybe don't yet trust in the process, or don't yet believe in the outcomes, or are just inherently suspicious of the field in which they've perceived as EG marketing communications, will always look at what we do and think, "Well, it's probably good, but I don't think it's worth the money because I can't afford it at the moment." And that can be really disheartening.

Deep down, the one thing that they don't want to articulate is that they can't afford to do the thing. My point is to not be distracted by that, to not allow yourself to have your energy drained by bad faith. Rather than beating ourselves up or squeezing down what we offer, trust in the value of what we offer.

29

Create Strong Pillars

"Give away your best information.
Building this trust with prospects will result in
bigger financial returns than bland content."
~Stacey Kehoe

When I was working in the corporate world, I went out of my way to get on the right side of the following people from day one in my jobs: the receptionist, the security guards, the post team, and the bosses' secretaries. The receptionist would have my back if I was running late. We didn't want people seeing one another as they arrived and left the building.

In my late twenties to early thirties, I worked for the UK's first interactive television station. During the planning stages of our launch, we were looking for a fresh marketing and media agency to help us publicise the platform and get UK consumers onboard and buying through it.

We invited several agencies to pitch. I got a call one day from our receptionist asking me to come down as soon as I could. Thinking there was something wrong, I immediately headed downstairs to the ground floor.

A sprightly courier was there, bag across his chest (classic) with a big grin on his face. On the floor at his feet, he had a small television set, and in his right hand, a sledgehammer. Interesting! He proceeded to smash the television in front of us—the receptionist was horrified! WHAT a mess! I was perplexed and felt it was a waste of a good television. Anyway, apparently the courier had been dispatched with the message of "Work with us—we'll help you to excite UK consumers to smash their perception of a television set as a passive tool and replace it with all the marvellous possibilities offered by interactive television." It was a neat idea—but they didn't get it.

The post team always kept an eye out for the urgent letters or internal memos that I was looking out for. When I started working, we would put internal memos into large envelopes and distribute them around the building via our postal teams. Each envelope was reusable and 'sealed' using an attached string around a circular disc at the back. In the interest of saving trees, they could be used up to fifty times. Each time I went to send a message/internal memo to 'Graham Green' I would add his name in the next box that was unfilled, making sure I'd crossed out my name as the recipient above.

The bosses' secretaries, they were the world's best gatekeepers, still are. Always so professional and friendly, but nonetheless, the gatekeepers. Befriending them and showing empathy always helped to get me higher up the queue than those who blatantly tried to go round them.

Today, as a business owner, it's a very different story. The foundational pillars will be a great commercial lawyer, a proactive, down-to-earth, can-do type accountant. A good VA who will support your growth (when you are ready).

You will need coaches of different types throughout your career: business coaches, sales coaches, social media coaches, book coaches. As soon as you start using consultants and working with people, get a good HR consultant onboard—or at least start to build that relationship. HR is a strategic pillar and just as important as the accountant and lawyer. If you are a solopreneur, that pillar will come later, and trust me, they will help to protect you and your business as it grows.

Once you have your foundations in place, it's time to build then next level of support.

Keep evaluating what you are doing vs. tasks that are taking too long and/or that you don't enjoy. It's often these tasks that can be outsourced.

A great question to ask yourself is, if I could get two to three hours back, what would that enable me to do and how would that accelerate my business growth?

30

Power of Your Network

"Choose co-founders the way you would choose a spouse."
~Danielle Newnham (entrepreneur and author)

Bill Hewlett and David Packard first became friends after they had graduated from Stanford, way back in 1934. Having both graduated with electrical engineering degrees, they rented a garage in Palo Alto and started to work on their first product. By 1939, they decided to formally go into partnership. Do you know how they decided what name came first? By flipping a coin.

Danielle Weisberg and Carly Zakin, co-founders of TheSkimm, met one another while studying abroad in Rome and had a shared love of fried artichokes. Today, it has over 1.5 million subscribers and brought in roughly $20 million of revenue in 2019.

Some may say destiny had a part to play in how they met—that may well be. The point is, there was still an element of networking in their meeting.

In today's world, a lot of us hustle daily—seven days a week—creating content, getting content created for us, showing up at in-person networking, digital networking. It's exhausting—and necessary.

We have built up an extensive network on LinkedIn over the last two years and will continue to invest our time, effort, and money on building that.

Focusing on exactly *who* you want to be talking to via networking can be incredibly powerful and lead to big client wins and partnerships. It is all in the planning. We've got some clients who plan their content one month in advance; others prefer to do it once a week.

Providing *value* to your network is critical (and that's different, by the way, than giving things away). Interacting, by being curious, you can create a brand for you and your business that generates revenue.

It takes time. Don't expect that to happen overnight. Your engaged network becomes a community who will support you, get to know you, keep you front of mind, and recommend you to others. A lot of whom you may never even meet.

The principle to building a great network is to work out what is going to be mutually beneficial, maintaining that authenticity (which isn't easy), and turning up. Consistency is a powerful thing.

Authenticity is a scary thing, believe me. There are enough keyboard warriors and trolls out there who just can't wait to spread their negativity. It's hard to not take it personally. That authenticity, however, can lead to brilliant things happening for you in your networking and open up new, and often unexpected, doors.

Let me give you an example. As a post-menopausal, middle-aged, pale but not so stale female, I regularly talk about my experiences with menopause, how I no longer recognise my body, and am ashamed of it and my hair loss.

Many women have reached out. We've got to talking and they are now huge advocates for our business, and even our clients.

Go network your heart out—and have a plan. It's a campaign that needs to give you a decent ROI, after all.

31

Competition – Friend or Foe?

*"Anyone who imagines they can work alone winds up
surrounded by nothing but rivals, without companions.
The fact is, no one ascends alone."*
~Lance Armstrong

"I'd prefer to work with you as opposed to having to constantly wonder what you're up to." A few years ago, I decided to get over myself and collaborate with someone who I saw as a competitor.

You know that fight or flight? Well I was always the fighter up until that point. I learned a valuable lesson: we were far stronger together than we were by being distracted by fighting one another. I mean, who knew?

I have built up several strong collaborations with other business coaches, those who share my passion, have my authenticity, and my desire to genuinely change the lives of founders and their families by helping them to be successful on their terms.

What's the other trait we all have? We are all mightily curious. I mean ridiculously so. We've got the confidence to ask those difficult questions as I touched on in an earlier chapter.

The bottom line to collaborating with those in your field is that you have a mutual respect. Of course, there is always going to be an element of risk. That would be no different than if you had an employee. Having weighty NDAs in place is one way to keep things official.

My point is, it's easier to succeed and grow a business with a team. In fact, it's only then that you become *a business.*

Sadly, there have been instances, albeit rarely, where my clients have had to exercise their rights within an NDA because a collaborator walked off with a client or used their IP without their prior consent. So yes, it does happen. That's the reality of any business, right? We all have problems that we need to deal with and overcome. And learn from.

Just to reiterate: ***if the business is solo reliant on you, you are still an employee***. Having a support team in place means *the business* can still make money, even if you are off on your holiday.

Notice how I went from working with the competition at the beginning of this chapter to collaborating a couple of paragraphs in. That's the journey I've been on. I feel far lighter. I no longer compare what I am doing to what others in my field are doing. I OWN my space, how we serve our clients, and the results and outcomes we achieve.

I feel so much more uplifted and lighter because I'm focusing on collaboration as opposed to competition. I'm not a tree-hugging, hairy-footed pansy. I'll still use my fight, and I'll use it in the right way—and only when provoked!

32

Beware the Smoke and Mirrors

"It's a highly deceptive world, one that constantly asks you to comment but doesn't really care what you have to say."
~David Levithan

How many times have you gone onto social media and seen someone that looks like they are more successful than you?

We *all* compare ourselves to others, so it's a conscious decision not to. The number of times I 'scratch under the surface' by asking my curious questions, I find out that it's a very different story. It's very much a 'fake it until you make it' kind of thing.

The smoke and mirrors can work both ways, and I am going to give you an example of both so you can decide for yourself how you want to play it.

Many years ago, when building a PR firm with a great friend of mine, we organised a reception at a large hotel in London. I invited a potential client who asked if they could bring along someone I would 'find interesting.' My curiosity was piqued!

Along came Georgie. Originally from Scotland, she had a thriving business. In all honesty, I can't quite remember what she did. It was how she made it that has stayed with me for more than twenty years.

She still had a fledgling business. In fact, she had sunk most of her money into her venture and was close to going bust. She had one last ditch effort that she wanted to try and pull off. She arranged an event a bit like ours and hired a handful of actors. She trained them all on what she did for a living, how her business benefited others. On the night of the event, she said she was inwardly petrified, she hadn't paid off the event, and, frankly, she didn't have the money to do so if it didn't work.

The actors did their part and mingled among the guests. They kept mental notes of who was whom and asked all the questions that Georgie had asked of them.

After the event, she had enough leads from the work of the actors that night and their thorough debrief to her afterwards that she was able to close a significant amount of business and got out of her predicament. It was a brave move, a really brave move, and I've never heard of anything quite like it since. It was a smoke and mirrors scenario—on speed!

Now let's look at another scenario where it didn't go so well. More recently, I was talking to a would-be partner who had always given us the perception of being a big business. At least bigger than we first thought. The reason why that mattered to me was because I needed a larger organisation that had its own staff for a particular project. If I was going to hire a firm, and then they hired out to other associates or consultants—that was an expensive project for my client—and not right in my book.

I quickly found out that all the staff were associates—and 'all the staff' meant they had one associate. Their turnover was $12K—I'm not sure how they were surviving. Instead of them gaining new work, we ended up taking them on as a client and have subsequently helped them grow to have a full-time team of six with ten additional associates. So now we can utilise their services should the same scenario arise in the future.

Had they done anything wrong? Absolutely not. They simply hadn't got some of their foundational work done: a clear pricing structure, an understanding of exactly what they offered, and who they helped. As a result, when someone like us came along who they wanted to work with and started asking all sort of questions, they simply weren't ready as there was a huge disconnect between perception and reality. We could hire our own associate. We were looking for a quicker fix in hiring specific talent that was employed elsewhere so it was cost effective for our client.

Anyway, the outcome for them was that it was bad for their immediate bank balance and bad for a brand reputation. No matter how small, we all have a brand and a reputation to uphold.

Be careful. If you are going to use those smoke and mirrors and fake it until you make it, use it wisely because it might just backfire on you.

33

When One Door Closes,

Another Will Open

"Realize that if a door closed,
it's because what was behind it wasn't meant for you."
~Mandy Hale

During my early twenties, I had planned a two-week vacation to Sydney, Australia. My boss at the time offered his chauffeur services to take me to the airport. Of course, that's something I wasn't going to turn down!

There was significant roadworks on the M25 during that time. For those of you who aren't from the UK, the M25 is the road. Of. Horrors. It's like the roads around LA—always gridlocked and you forever find yourself looking around a sea of other stationary vehicles, asking yourself, "Why does this always happen to me?"

Anyway, we got to the airport so early that when I went to check in, the lady at the Cathy Pacific desk asked if I could do them a favour and take an earlier flight. I was slightly reluctant as it meant I had a longer transfer time in Hong Kong.

Then she said those magic words: "We will, of course, upgrade you to business class for no extra charge." Sold!

I boarded that flight with the biggest grin on my face. I was fortunate to be sitting next to a really interesting lady, and we lightly chatted until just before we were due to descend into Kowloon airport. (Yes, that's a long time ago now as Kowloon was shut many years ago.)

She signalled for the air steward, who came over. Up until that point, we had had remarkable service and I simply put it down to the fact that we were in business class. It turned out that my travel companion was the wife of a senior pilot. She'd signalled the steward over to ask if anyone was in the jump seat for landing. They weren't.

I was escorted up to the cockpit and went through the pleasantries with the captain and co-pilot, and watched with wonder and awe as they brought the plane down to land with the wings almost kissing those high rises on the descent.

Sadly, the days of being able to sit in a jump seat are long gone. It was one of those once-in-a-lifetime experiences for me. I love travel, particularly flying, so it was a dream come true.

What's this got to do with one door closing and another opening? If I hadn't taken that offer of an earlier flight, I would never have met that lady and had that experience. I was open to a new opportunity, and by being open, it's incredible what can happen.

The same can be said for one door closing and another opening. Everything happens for a reason and sometimes, no matter how hard you try, that door isn't going to budge. Step back, look around you, clear your mind, and be open to that new opportunity that is just around the corner.

One of our team first came to us as a marketing specialist. He worked exceptionally hard, and we got on really well. One day, he explained that marketing wasn't his bag and that he found it soul-destroying. The daily hustle, the long hours, the stillness of being in front of a screen all day. He'd previously been a PT and wanted to go back to that. Cue his first client—me! To this day, he keeps me accountable and in check. As a real foodie, I LOVE my food—so does my expanding waistline.

He has also started to learn the wonderful world of NFTs and digital currencies, and we are exploring that together. He is building up two incomes—clever chap. I believe that is the future, having multiple incomes.

It really is true what they say, as one door closes, another one will open—you won't know where and you certainly won't know when. Just be sure that it will.

34

Why a No Is Better Than a Maybe

"If someone does not appreciate you, let them go.
They need to learn lessons that you cannot teach them."
~Wayne Gerard Trotman

Getting a maybe can kill a business. Especially if the potential buyer is an amiable person who doesn't want to hurt your feelings but simply won't commit.

It can mislead you into spending more time on what you think is a prospect: your energy, your attention, and your cost of sale. Which will all be in vain as they really want to say no. That's why a 'maybe' can kill a business. It can also mean you lose legitimate business as you are too busy looking in the wrong direction.

Get to a yes or no quickly and move on. There are three reasons for a no: finance, fit, or future.

If it's finance and they can't afford you yet, how can you stay connected without that taking up too much of your time? Think about putting in a call every quarter or sending a personalized email to stay in touch.

If it's fit, then it's a case of moving on quickly as it simply won't work. Sometimes people are just not the right fit. They aren't going to get on with each other. It's okay to wish them well and move on.

If it's no right now—then when could it be a yes in the future? That's up to you to decide how often you reconnect and what value you share with them over time. For example: I have sent articles or information about relevant events that I knew would be of interest. That way, I stayed front of mind without being an annoying would-be supplier.

By you saying no and you receiving a no, it shows respect. As William Ury, Ph.D. wrote in his book *The Power of a Positive No* says, "You give respect to the other not so much because of who *they* are but because of who *you* are. *Respect is an expression of yourself and your values.*"

Do I like it when I get a no from an organisation wanting to work with us? No, of course not. As much as I like to think I have my ego in check, it still stings when I get a no. As soon as I get a no, I take action and move on to work on other leads with empowerment and focus. However, I will always analyse what could we do better next time and take that learning to improve what we offer and how we communicate that every day. So that no? It can be one of the best lessons you have. That maybe is simply far too costly for so many businesses.

35

Art of Selling Without Selling

"We each sell a little piece of happiness.
You are elevating someone's spirit in some way,
and to do that you have to understand the source of their angst
and then you have to frame your product as a solution."
~Sonia Marciano

What happens to your brain when you need to go out there to sell your services or product? Some people love it, others really don't. They seize up, start using big words, and going into some robotic mantra.

In these next few sections, we look at how to sell, ask open questions to get to the heart of the issues facing your prospect or client, and the importance of rewind and playback.

Let's look at the art of selling. Firstly, you don't have to sell. How does that make you feel when I say that? Better? Relieved? Disappointed if you are a sales' junky?

Most of us will ask a friend of a loved one if they fancy going to the cinema to see that latest film or try out that new restaurant that's just opened downtown. You've just sold a concept or an idea.

195

We all sell each and every day—we simply don't label it as such.

Let's look at it slightly differently. How many years of experience have you got? How much have you invested to get to your level of expertise? What difference will your service or product make to a business, or to someone? How will they benefit and what are the outcomes you can give them that they are unable to obtain without your services?

So, you see, you don't actually sell. You are here to serve and help others. In his book *To Sell Is Human*, Dan Pink indicates that more than 40% of our professional time is spent selling.

I object to those blatant pitches that slide into my DMs. You know the ones I mean, where they clearly have spent no time looking at what we do and offer and are wanting to inflict their pitch on me. A real plug and play just doesn't work.

When I met my coach at a networking event in Canada, she never once sold to me. She asked me a lot of questions about our business, our ambitions, and our goals for the next couple of years. Then she asked about our challenges.

She shared case studies with me about other women founders who were just like me: ambitious, dedicated to serving others, and wanting to make a life-changing impact on their lives.

We agreed to have a follow-up call, during which she got straight to the point, explained they had another cohort coming up in the next few weeks, and asked if I would like to join.

I couldn't join that specific one; however, I did join the one after that. At no point did she pitch me or try to close me. She asked me all the right questions about my business. She was interested and demonstrated that she had gotten great results for founders just like me.

The most powerful question, once you've established their needs and desires is, "Would you like my help?"

Now you're in a selling conversation, not a pitch session.

36

Read the Room

"I believe luck is preparation meeting opportunity.
If you hadn't been prepared when the opportunity came along,
you wouldn't have been lucky."
~Oprah Winfrey

The two most overly used words in my vocabulary are 'how' and 'why.' I can't help it!

When it comes to preparing for meetings and attending sales meetings, be that in person or virtually, being able to read the room, and read it well, comes from great preparation.

During one particularly competitive tender process, the company I was representing had six other consultancies they were talking to and five decision makers in the room who then needed to go through a procurement process. It was complicated.

To read that room, we needed to be better prepared than any other company who was pitching that day. I personally contacted each person who was attending our initial meeting, got to understand *their* agenda, what they wanted to get out of a relationship with the supplier, and the role they played. I also found out if they had any of their recommended consultancies in the mix. In that way, I would get a better reading of who we needed to work extra hard on to get on our side.

The common frustration or weak spot for them was procurement. The procurement department was particularly diligent by all accounts, but it took a lot of effort and paperwork to onboard a new supplier. Time was of the essence in this instance, and we came up with a way round this problem, even before we got to the initial pitch with them.

We went into the first meeting ahead of the competition. We'd built the relationships, we'd solved a collective problem, and we'd demonstrated we were on their side. We'd got that room all mapped out, even before we got there.

When there is more than one decision maker, it's a complicated process to win a piece of business. That preparation is absolutely critical.

In other situations, it can be much simpler and can lead to some interesting conversations.

I recently met a potential collaborative partner over lunch. We'd been introduced via a mutual friend and I was keen to find out more about them. On doing my research, they offered complimentary services to us in regions that we hadn't yet had any success across Europe.

During the meeting, it was clear that our potential collaboration partner could also do with our help. I didn't want to push it and side-track the meeting.

I left my questioning about their needs until the end. Then I asked a flurry of questions about who they'd like to work with and how we might be able to support them in selling at a great value through our coaching program. I found out that they had a big pitch coming up and they really wanted to win the client. Now this was getting even more exciting.

By listening earlier on in the meeting, I was able to establish a great rapport, start to build trust that takes time to develop in any relationship, and demonstrate our results by sharing some of our case studies from our recent client work.

It worked. I walked away that day with an invitation to a podcast interview in front of a big audience, an outline for a joint program that we could roll out together, and a new client.

Listen to your instinct and listen with your curiosity. There's a big difference between listening to learn something and listening to respond.

It's all in the questioning, so let's talk a bit more about those powerful open questions.

37

What Does an Open Question

Really Mean?

*"When you sincerely want to connect on deeper levels
and encourage other people to talk about themselves,
use open-ended questions to stimulate your conversation
and get the ball rolling."*
~Susan C. Young

See what I did there? That's an open question right there. An open question is asking the recipient to respond with more than a 'yes' or 'no' answer. Why is that important when you are trying to build that rapport?

Well, if you are asking a question relating to their needs and building up to being able to discuss how you can best support them, a no is hard to overturn to a yes. Can it be done? Of course—it just takes more work.

I have a loose questioning infrastructure that I have in my mind for every meeting. Over and above my own research. These simple yet powerful questions can make all the difference.

My opening questions are along these lines:

- "What you like to achieve by the end of this meeting?"

- "How can we best make use of the time you have today?"

- "What would you like me to share with you?"

- "What would success look like at the end of this meeting?"

That gives me a clear understanding of their agenda. Great. Now to get into it.

My aim is to gather information, to find out more about their challenges and their perceived challenges. These aren't always the same, and it's worth bearing that in mind. Earlier in my career, I got stung a couple of times by thinking I knew what the challenges were of a business and how I could help. What I discovered, in fact, was that I knew the person's challenges I met with, and that can be different from what the company needs.

The art of truly understanding what they want is to rewind and playback. Let me explain this in more detail in the next section. Before I do that, here's a list of some other open questions to consider.

Openers and big picture:
- What's the plan for this year?

- What are you most proud of so far this year?

- What's working well for you right now?

- What's not?

- What's the impact of leaving this?

Risk/problems:

- What's the risk to you and the business if you don't do anything about XYZ?

- What's the risk to you and the business if you stay as is?

- What skills do you have in-house to address this?

- Where are the gaps?

Existing providers/suppliers

- How would you rate your existing suppliers?

- What's working well with them?

- What's not? Where are the gaps?

- What would success look like for you?

- What are the must-haves?

- What are the nice-to-haves?

Service provider (relationship):

- How do you see this working?

- Who would we be reporting to?

- What's important to them?

Success:

- What does success look like to you?

- By when?

- How far up the agenda is this as a priority for the company?

- What could get in the way of that success?

- How will you/we measure that success?

Timings

- By when are you looking to make a decision?

- How can we best support you in this?

There are obviously many, many other questions I ask. I hope this gives you a better understanding of open questioning and will help you to prepare for your next new business meeting. Let's get on that rewind and playback.

38

Rewind and Playback

"Most people do not listen with the intent to understand;
they listen with the intent to reply."
~Stephen R. Covey

"What I'm hearing is…" is a classic rewind and playback technique designed to help the person you are meeting with to know that you are listening to them and, in some instances, realise that perhaps what they think is a good idea possibly isn't. I call it the 'unicorn scenario.'

It also means that you truly understand their needs and the situation. It will help you to bridge during the meeting and think real time about the gaps in your questioning.

Always give a playback summary at the end of every meeting and start to playback at least ten minutes before the end of the meeting. This will also give you to time to ask and receive any final questions and to agree next steps.

Here's an example of one I used recently on an existing client during one of our coaching sessions:

"What I'm hearing is that you'd like to rollout your workshops in September of this year. Is that right, Sally?"

"Yes," Sally replied. "Gosh, that's not long, is it? I haven't even got my concepts together for what I want to deliver. Come to think about it, I haven't done any market research to see if anyone wants the damn thing yet or not."

By metaphorically putting the mirror up and reflecting what she had just told me, she'd gained an important insight. Whilst she wanted to do one thing, she had no idea if it was the right thing to do or not.

Give it a go in your next meeting, and remember to reflect afterwards on what worked well and what didn't. Out of that, you will also get a better understanding of how you will use this technique differently in your next meeting.

39

A No Today Could Be a Yes Tomorrow

"Judge a man by his questions rather than by his answers."
~Voltaire

None of us like it when a client says no. However, as we talked about in an earlier chapter, it's far better to get a no than a maybe.

A no isn't always a permanent no. Remember the part where we said there were three types of nos? Fit, finance, or future.

This one's all about the future. When a client chooses to go with another supplier, there is more than likely a contract that's in place with whom they've chosen to go with. That might be for a year, two years, three even. The challenge will always be if that contract has an exclusivity clause in it. For this scenario, I'm working on the premise that this is so. Whilst I can't touch the client whilst in contract, I can certainly bide my time and use it wisely.

My point is, a lot can change in that contracted period, and by building a relationship with the client you (temporarily) lost to, albeit loosely, you can potentially win down the line.

We won a such a new client two months ago. It had been a company that turned me down just over two years ago. We were still building our reputation at that time, and still are today; however, we had fewer case studies, we didn't have the following we have now, and the brand was in its infancy.

I took it upon myself to regularly add thoughtful comments to their posts on LinkedIn. I knew they shared my fascination with all things neuroscience, and so I would share interesting articles with them or new book suggestions.

I got a call out of the blue at the beginning of 2022 asking if we could talk.

At no point did I ask them how it was going with the existing supplier they had chosen to go with or what was working well with them or not. I rose above all of that and kept firmly on their radar and tried to find ways of adding value.

So you see, a no today doesn't always mean it's going to be a no tomorrow. Keep at it—it just might pay off in the longer term for you.

Part 3:

Succeed

40

Live Your Future Now

"The future depends on what you do today."
~Mahatma Gandhi

What do you want you and your business to look like in ten years' time? What will that give you? What will that mean for you and your family? Can you paint that picture in your head and bring it to life?

Capture that in a way that works best for you. Maybe you will create a mood board that you put over your desk that you can see each day, or a screen saver on your laptop or phone. It's a start. It's still intangible, still an aspiration, so let's MAKE it happen.

Build your business on positive energy and not from a place of scarcity. If you are building your business because you don't want to be XYZ, that's a lot of pressure and creates a negative vibe. You are holding yourself back and creating problems from your past and allowing them to continually tell you subconsciously why you can't do it, which will impact your future.

Let's look at that one slightly differently. What are you hoping to give others through your work? Where's the joy in it? The energy that comes out of that is empowering, it's uplifting—and it's life changing.

Now, use that positive energy to look at your future, *really* see it, *really* feel it. What will you be doing on the weekends to relax? I want you to really bring it to life and train your brain and mind in new ways to facilitate where you want to be—and *who* you want to be.

I'm a massive fan of the work of Dr. Joe Dispenza. In his book *Breaking the Habit of Being Yourself*, he writes about how we can change. In one section of his book, he discusses Survival vs. Creation. "To initiate this step of creation, it is always good to move into a state of wonder, contemplation, possibility, reflection, or speculation, by asking yourself some important questions. Open-ended inquiries are the most provocative approach to producing a fluent stream of consciousness:

- What would it be like to…?
- What is a better way to…?
- What if I was the person living in this reality?
- Who in history do I admire, and what were his/her admirable traits?

The answers that come will naturally form a new mind, because as you sincerely respond to them, your brain will begin to work in new ways. By beginning to mentally rehearse new ways of being, you start

214

rewiring yourself neurologically to a new mind. The more you can "re-mind" yourself, the more you'll change your brain and life."

Powerful stuff, right? Live your future self today. You'll be amazed at what you can achieve.

EXERCISE:

Here's a great exercise to really get you using future back thinking. This is simply when there is no data available to us (most of us use present forward thinking).

Use this template to help you to plan your business ten years from now. Take your time and keep it safe—it will evolve and develop over the coming years.

PUTTING IT INTO BOXES

A simple way to break it down RUDE

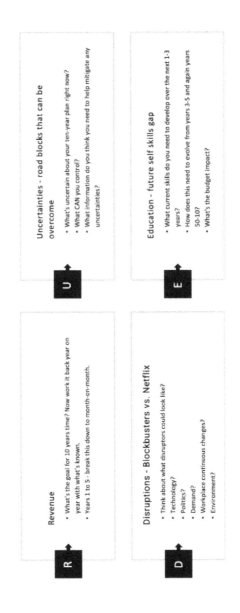

R

Revenue
- What's the goal for 10 years time? Now work it back year on year with what's known.
- Years 1 to 5 - break this down to month-on-month.

U

Uncertainties - road blocks that can be overcome
- What's uncertain about your ten-year plan right now?
- What CAN you control?
- What information do you think you need to help mitigate any uncertainties?

D

Disruptions - Blockbusters vs. Netflix
- Think about what disruptors could look like?
- Technology?
- Politics?
- Demand?
- Workplace continuous changes?
- Environment?

E

Education - future self skills gap
- What current skills do you need to develop over the next 1-3 years?
- How does this need to evolve from years 3-5 and again years 50-10?
- What's the budget impact?

Interlude

An Interview with Adam Durant

Sam:

When I was a little girl, my dad had worked hard to build up his own business. He surrounded himself with other businesspeople who all shared their experiences with one another. He built a formidable team and continued to earn their loyalty.

There are key people you need around you when building any business. One of them is most definitely a great bank manager. There are very few banks that offer national support with a personal service.

I have always been impressed by Metro Bank, they champion the small business owner. They care, I mean genuinely care.

I was lucky enough that the brilliant Adam Durrant said yes to an interview. As always, he was insightful, and I have broken our conversation down into sections – pure gold! I hope you enjoy reading this as much as I enjoyed talking to him.

A Bit About Metro Bank and What Makes Them Different

Metro Bank began in 2010, when it launched its first store, really from nothing. We had to help the regulators write a new banking licence, because it hadn't been done for 140 years, roughly. The records aren't even old enough to tell us exactly when.

There's a gentleman from America, Vernon Hill, who brought the model from the US to the UK and the model is very, very simple. It's convenience banking. It's seven days a week. It's thinking like retailers do in the current day. Everything is instant and then seven days a week. It just so happens that we do banking business, commercial, retail, whatever it may be. So 2010 July, we opened Holborn Store (London) Number One. We are just on the cusp of launching store number 79 up in Leicester on the 25th of February. It's been an amazing story, an incredible journey.

Twelve years this July will be the journey of building those 79 stores, not far from three million customers, about 4500 colleagues. As I say, our 79 stores include Amaze Direct sites, which are our contact centers, but we call them Amaze Direct because that's where we look to amaze customers on the telephone, as well as in our 79 stores.

Nearly 12 years on, we built a bank that was the first to the High

Street. There are many other fintechs, other banks that have come out there, which is great, gives customers choice and particularly business owners choice.

If you go back to the idea started 2008, when Vernon Hill came to the UK and thought that there wasn't much choice. Look at America. There are something like 3000 different banks that you can choose from. You go back to the UK 2008, 2009. There were realistically five, maybe six you could choose from. We look to give customers another choice.

Vernon Hill

He was the chairman and founder of Metro Bank. He launched it with a gentleman called Craig Donaldson, who was the chief executive at the time. Vernon had launched a bank in the States. In the early seventies, built it from his first store to nearly 500. Again, that model was very, very similar, if not the same as Metro Bank. It was based on seven days a week. It had "drive-thru stores" as we call them. We've got a few now in the UK and yeah, it works. The model is growing.

What are the common pitfalls that small business owners can avoid?

"First and foremost, to anyone that does run their own business because it is tough. We all know the stats of how many businesses after year one or two don't quite succeed, because it is incredibly tough.

I noticed that many people are very good at what they do, whether it be painting, decorating, web design, doesn't matter what it is. Their expertise in the business is there and undoubted. It's all the other things like, invoicing, bookkeeping, marketing, business development, developing the business in the first place?

First and foremost, you can't do everything. So don't expect that you can. Ideally, get good people around you. It could be friends, could be family, could be people you've worked with in the past, but don't be afraid to delegate some of the stuff that you do.

If you're starting a business, what do you want to actually achieve? Financial gain requires a number of customers, or a certain number of widgets that you want to sell. Know what "good" looks like.

A lot of people we see in the banking world that are starting, obviously need a bank account for their new business. We ask, "What do the next 12 months look like?"

"I don't really know."

"Well, if you don't really know, you don't know whether you've been a success or not. You need to drill it down to what do I need to survive? Then work it from the end backwards, if you like, if that makes it slightly easier."

A lot of people, when they start business, they don't split their business and their personal banking. They think, "I'll just add it to my existing personal bank account." That just muddies the waters. You can't then see which are business expenses and which are personal expenses. That may make it tricky when you get to do your end-of-year accounts. Definitely split your banking.

A lot of people do that, I think, because they think business banking means there's going to be a cost. They need to watch the cost when starting a business, which you absolutely do. But business banking doesn't have to cost you any money. If it does, it may be very, very little as your business starts. Then as it grows, there may be other elements of it. That's why I say talk to a bank, talk to someone that you know, talk to someone you've got a relationship with, and just understand what options are there.

The other bit that's interesting, and maybe because it's been a tough couple of years, but when you start a business, you need some cash to start that business. We speak to a lot of people in banking, in what 22 years I've been in it now, and people say, "I'm starting a business, can I borrow some money?" We say, "Well no." They look at us and say, "Why not? I'm starting a business. I need…" whatever amount of money it might be. It might be a 100 pounds, might be 100,000 pounds. It doesn't matter. When you're starting your own business, it is risky. You are taking a big risk in your life.

But banks will say, "Well, we don't know what the future looks like," because like anything, when you have a credit score as an individual, banks will look backwards and then try and guess what's going to happen moving forward. For a business that's just starting, nobody can look backwards because you don't have any history and therefore working out what the future look like is very, very difficult.

If you want to start a business and you need some funds to do it, then look at the funds you've got yourself. Look at friends and family that are willing to support you because the idea you've got is the real magic. If you need some funds to make that happen, borrowing money from a bank is probably going to add more pressure to that than you need when you're starting out.

What are the right questions to ask when it comes to banking needs?

Really good question. I speak to a lot of customers and when I ask them, "What do you need?" they usually say, "I just need a bank account." They very much see it similar to their personal banking.

When you look at a business bank, understand how you want to connect, how you want to speak to your bank, how you want to transact on a daily basis. Understand how you want to keep an eye on your banking every single day.

What technology does the bank have that you are going to need? Most banks broadly, a bank account is a very, very similar product. It's the other things on the outside of it that make life easier running a business.

If you need an app to check in every single morning, if that's your routine and you need to understand where the finances are, which is a good habit to have, make sure the app you log into fits your lifestyle. If it's a quick glance and nothing else, if it's a transaction every day you need to do, make sure the technology that the bank has fits your purpose.

I'll use an example: at Metro Bank, when we're onboarding personal business customers or commercial customers, we very much look at it as we are applying to the customer to win their business, please come and bank with us. These are the reasons why. This is what we'll do for you. Now we understand you. This is what's happening.

What some other banks do is they turn the tables and say, "Well, Mr. Customer, convince me why we should let you bank with us." That's a very, very different model.

I spend a lot of my time understanding the individual, the business, what they do, how they operate and then say, "Well, actually with what you've said, we could do this for you." The technology that the bank has available at your fingertips is a big, big part of it. There are loads of other things coming down the line. We've got the Capability and Innovation Fund, which lets us add technology. One we've done recently is the ability for a customer to send an invoice to their client directly from the app. Imagine you're out there with the customer. You might be delivering work or quoting, but you can just send an invoice in a couple of clicks and then it reconciles it coming back in. So again, that's time saving for the business owner.

The other things they need to ask the bank for is point of contact. What makes Metro Bank different is that every single business customer has a relationship manager.

You may be a startup business that doesn't know what the future looks like because it is brand new. You might be a very mature business, been running for 20, 30, 40 years. Doesn't matter to Metro Bank. You have a relationship manager, which means you've got a mobile number, you've got an email address, you know where they're based. They're normally in your local store, in your local community.

Ideally, they are well-connected individuals as well. You may need to know someone for your business from the local council or the local business improvement district or an accountant to help you out or something. Our relationship managers are in the community and well-connected.

Our business customers, when they come and start a business, they may say, "I never need to come into my branch. I never need to speak to my relationship manager. I'm very self-sufficient. I just need the online ability."

That's great, but you may, at one point, need that relationship manager. Knowing who they are is one thing, the ability to contact them is another. Again, that's how we are very, very different at Metro Bank. I spend, and it sounds like I do no work, but a lot of my time just having a coffee with business customers every week. I find that refreshing and almost old-fashioned banking, but with really modern technology.

What other events have you run to support small businesses?

We do so many events at Metro Bank. Over the last couple of years, we've done a lot of virtual, which I'm sure we're all familiar with.

One of the things we do, in terms of physical space, are big, high ceilings. Floor space is huge in our stores. We offer them to local networking groups, individual businesses to use. We'd have normal business customers coming in and out, and then we'd have a section of the store that people could host, display their business, promote their business. People come together, the local professionals in the area, to coffee, have a glass of wine, and just talk and network.

I hosted one a week before last with the Northwest London Chamber. They did a lot of the admin for us. We invited guests, they invited guests, and it was very much just an opportunity to come for the evening, there was a lady there that just started a business with some vegan chocolate. She had a little stall there, and we were just having a conversation over a glass of wine, a few chocolates, and getting to know some people in the business arena.

Local events like that, we do on a regular basis across all 79 of our stores. We have done loads of things in the local community. We do a lot of events with local schools and deliver our Money Zone Program.

So that, in essence, is financial education to children. That gets us connected with the parents who may be running their own business. We do lots and lots of different things in any way that we can to support communities.

One of the things we did last year was our first ever marketing campaign at the bank. Generally, what we've done in the 11 years prior is really promote the culture of the ethos of Metro Bank, what we stand for in terms of custom convenience and creating fans.

Last year, slight tilt on that. We focused on business customers and the best place to do that. We wanted to make sure everyone knows that Metro Bank is very much a business and commercial bank, as well as retail. The best way to do that, we felt, was going to speak to our existing business customers. We went to our local relationship managers in all the stores and said, "Have you got any great businesses, one that are willing to be in front of a camera?" Because it's not easy for everybody. Secondly, it's a chance for them to promote their business on the radio and in our advertising campaigns.

We had a fantastic young guy that had launched a business making fashionable prosthetics. If you wanted it to match your favorite pair of jeans or your favorite jumper or whatever, he would make it blend in with the fashion that you had and the style that you wanted. We got this guy to be part of an advertising campaign and promote his product on the radio. He talked about the relationship with us as his business bank at Metro Bank, how that helped him and his business.

We had another lady that was selling dog treats, and a guy that did vegan yogurts and food. All the businesses are fantastic. To this day, we are using their faces to promote what Metro Bank do.

How have you seen businesses change and evolve over the last couple of years?

Well, I think everybody has. We've certainly seen it the last two years. No one could ever plan for it. Businesses have evolved in so many different ways and it's been incredibly tough. Early on, I spoke to so many customers that were saying, "Adam, literally overnight, I've gone from being incredibly busy and successful. I generally don't know where my next opportunity to do what I do is going to come." I didn't know what to tell them because I didn't know either.

We've seen some businesses that were never selling online, maybe didn't have a landing page or website for their customers to even know what they do. Overnight, they were forced to have some online presence. That's opened up a world of opportunities whereby I could sell to people in a particular geography or particular post code. All of a sudden now, I've got the whole of the UK or even in some cases the whole of the world. Hospitality, food, restaurants was a great example. I spoke to loads of people that couldn't open their doors anymore, but then moved very quickly to a delivery format.

Have you got any innovations that you want to talk about?
The invoicing ability. First and foremost, there are loads at Metro Bank. We got a part of the Capability and Innovation Fund. In essence, it means that Metro Bank put some of their money in and the competition authority put some of their money in to make that competitiveness amongst the banks. That fund allows banks like us to invest in technology to make us attractive to businesses of all shapes and sizes. One of the things we've recently done is that invoice ability, based on feedback from our customers.

They can use the app whilst out with their customers, which is a very, very common way that people like to transact now and interact with the bank. A couple of clicks and you can send the invoice to that customer. Equally then, when the customer then pays you that money using the reference number or the invoice, it reconciles it all for you. Time saving for the customer, cost saving for the customer as well.

We're always looking at our ability to react quickly and support customers. We are very old-fashioned bankers in terms of relationship and conversation with the best technology and some business owners tell us quite a lot, "I miss the ability just to have a chat with my bank manager who knows me and my business and can make a decision."

A lot of that has been taken away. We've been investing in the last 3, 4, 6 months now and looking at the businesses, the accounts that they run with us, how they operate, and the external information that's there, and then making a lending decision to say, "If business ABC does need some support, can we do it and can we do it quickly?" Because like anything, we want something today.

A business owner doesn't want me to sit around for weeks and then say, "Oh, I'm really sorry. We can't do it." If I can tell you on the first day or very quickly, at least you know where you stand and you can then maybe look at other alternatives that are there. Maybe we can connect with other people that I know in my community that may be able to help this customer. There is always a way to get it done. It may not always be with your bank.

Then the final bit for us is just, as I mentioned earlier, we started in 2010. We've now got a team of in-house experts that can actually support business customers with the expertise to help them to trade internationally.

I had a guy that that was buying and selling plastics all around Africa. I connected him with our expert for trade finance. My customer had been in the industry for about 35, 40 years. After 45 minutes with our trade finance guy at Metro Bank, he said, "I wish I'd have met you 40 years ago because your knowledge is like nothing I've ever seen before."

What other human stories would you like to share?

I had a couple that were introduced to me through a guy that I used to work with at HSBC. He phoned me and said, "Look, Adam, I've got a couple of friends here that run fast food restaurants. They've got an opportunity to buy the free hold of one of the buildings that they run and operate." This couple moved to the UK from Sri Lanka about 25 years ago with literally nothing, and over the last 20 years, they built up one full restaurant and seven fast food ones.

He said, "Look, can you have a chat with them? They want a relationship with the bank. They've got an opportunity to buy one of the buildings that quite a well-known restaurant just vacated, and it was up for sale." I sat down and the first thing we always do is we just talk about the people behind the business. They sat there and said, "Oh, here's my financial."

I said, "Actually, I don't want to see that. I just want to know about you. Tell me your history. Where were you born? When did you come to the UK? You've got children? How old are they now? What school do they go to? How have you built up businesses that you have?"

I was just absolutely blown away by the hard work, the expertise of these individuals, and getting to know them and their family was important for us to decide, "Is this something we can support them with?"

I had gone from nothing to really, really successful. They were working all hours. Then they had the option to buy the building, which would save them some money. We built a very good story, by getting to know the individuals and focusing on what they've done and what they've built.

I talk to them regularly now, and that's the point. You get to know these people behind the business, which are the magic. They're the geniuses. We need to make what we do in banking world as simple as possible for them. That's what we've done.

Then the other story is a serial entrepreneur. I was introduced to this guy over three years ago because he was buying the master franchise for a children's education business in the UK. Again, I went to the meeting, didn't really know what I was walking into.

I knew it was a new startup, a bank account that he needed. Getting to know this particular individual and then asking a couple of questions led to, "I've also got this business, I've got plans to do this, and I've got plans to do the other." Again, I was just in awe of this individual.

I remember one of the things I said to him, "How many hours are there in your day? Because you've obviously got more than I have. The amount of things and businesses that you do." In addition to that, he's got three lovely young children that are all in education. There's homework and football classes and all the challenges that go with being a working parent. His wife also ran her own business and was just in the middle of setting up another gym that they were looking to launch. So again, just fascinating individual, incredibly hard-working family, and also incredibly ambitious to go on and develop other things.

It's just getting to know the people behind the business. When you ask for the financials, we're going to have to ask for all the terms and conditions to be agreed and so on, but that bit comes later. Get to know the people behind the business.

That means I'm going to ask you lots of questions, but I'd love to really just to get to know you, what makes you tick? What frustrates you? What things you do and don't like? Then we can work our way forward. Because it's a very, very honest relationship.

I'm talking to the same guy at 4:00 this afternoon. I talk to him regularly and we always make sure we can support each other. We're on WhatsApp, so if he needs anything, he just pings me a quick message. That goes back to the old-fashioned banking with a quick response for someone that you know, rather than an automated process. That's the beauty of my job.

41

Authenticity Matters

"Leaders should strive for authenticity over perfection."
~Sheryl Sandberg, Meta COO

What happens when you try and please everyone? You end up pleasing nobody and it can all fall apart.

Authenticity doesn't mean you have to bare your soul and deepest darkest secrets to the world. It's about being you when you turn up on social media, to your clients, stakeholders, and suppliers.

What matters to you? What values do you want the people you do business with to have? Note I said people and not businesses, because businesses are formed of a collective of people. They create the personality of a business and guide that institution through their own collection of values. As you will with your business.

Don't be afraid to say no to clients because they aren't aligned with what you think is important. That can weigh heavy with you over time and cause challenges down the line.

Let me give you an example: we won't work with organisations who are in it simply to make money. Where's the heart and soul in that?

Think about it for a minute: what's your 'hard no?' Who don't or won't you work with? How does that fit in with your authenticity?

We *will* work with founders who want to make a difference. Yes, there are over 14,700,000 companies out there who want to make that difference. We will work with them to define the outcome they will have on their clients.

Authenticity is also a huge employer branding benefit these days. BetterUp studied the positive impacts of inclusive leadership. A fundamental part to that inclusivity is authenticity.

From their research, they found seven key benefits. The following is taken from an article on their website:

Source: https://www.betterup.com/blog/authenticity-at-work

1.   140% increase in employee engagement.

2.   50% increase in team performance.

3.   90% increase in team innovation.

4.   54% lower turnover.

5.   150% increase in belonging.

6.   It helps people build their authentic personal brand.

7.   It helps people find their purpose — and live with greater purpose, clarity, and passion.

I used to use a 'work voice.' I thought it gave me greater credibility, but in fact, it had the opposite effect. People could spot it a mile off and couldn't connect with me.

Now? I'm happy to turn up as a slightly frumpy, middle-aged, post-menopausal woman who occasionally can turn the air a different shade of blue, with a real fire in my tummy for changing the lives of founders through a blend of coaching and consultancy, and to help them build a successful business on their terms. In fact, I have more energy now than I did twenty years ago and am more driven than ever before.

Authenticity is a powerful thing!

42

A Team of Many Forms

"Talent wins games, but teamwork and intelligence wins championships."
~Michael Jordan

At the start of 2020, I partnered with a firm in Egypt. One day, one of the partners said if it hadn't been for that year's chaos, it was highly likely that our partnership may not have been formed.

Sadly, that statement was true and led me to the realisation (as so many of us learned during that period of our lives) that we can find the right talent for our businesses anywhere in the world and from a more diverse background.

Today's people model for MindAbility came off the back of that profound conversation. I didn't want to employ full-time staff (at least not for the next few years). I also didn't want to employ people who were just like me. Diversity of thought is important to me. I want to be challenged. I want to learn from other people, every day if possible.

That is what I set out to find and am delighted with my team today. Jack and Hugo are a Godsend to me. They are two young men, living in Barcelona at present, who have the skills and experiences I don't have. They are living the dream as digital nomads, and, as a completely different generation, we learn a lot from one another. They call me out when I'm wrong—and I include them in a lot of my decision-making. What's the point of having that diversity of thought if I don't ask for it?

When you think about building your team or teams, think outside the box. You will be surprised at what you can find and what you can learn. Everyone benefits—especially your clients.

Make sure you do have a good HR consultant and a proactive accountant; they will help you to build a business using this model and protect you from unnecessary cross border taxes and potential employee/contractual challenges.

Interlude

An Interview with Lea Turner

Sam Eaton:

What's driven you to be as successful as you are?

Lea Turner:

It's weird to say successful because I still don't feel successful, and I think that's a running theme for a lot of people that are perceived as successful. I don't really know what successful is supposed to feel like. It's something in the distance that I'll eventually catch up to and suddenly one day I'll wake up feeling it.

I wouldn't say I was ever driven by money originally. When I started using LinkedIn, I was just trying to help my small business. And it was a very small business. I was making minimum wage. And then I started seeing other women, around my age, and they were striving. They were doing so well, and they were running their own companies. And I was like, "Hold on a minute. These women aren't smarter than me. These women aren't more privileged than I am. They'd have come from not dissimilar backgrounds. And yet look at them." And I thought, "Why not me?"

One of the answers that I've reflected on a lot over the last couple of years is I never knew it was possible. I went to school and school said, "You do your exams. You go to college, you go to university. You get a job." And that's what you do for the next 50 years until you retire. And then you claim your state pension and you die in a retirement village or something. And I was like, "That's just the path that you're on. That's the normal path."

The idea of having my own business never entered my mind. It just wasn't something that anybody ever said. And I didn't see anybody that was doing it. I didn't have people in my life that owned their own successful businesses. My grandparents had a post office, that was the closest I came. Everybody else just had jobs. I'm not saying there's anything wrong with having a job, but that was the only thing that I saw. They worked nine-to-five jobs. They came home, they didn't think about work. And then they went back to work in the morning, and they did something that they weren't really passionate about so that they could pay the bills.

And then I did start my own business, more through accident than intention. I had a side hustle just to make some extra money, and it was doing very well. I was earning as much as I was in my job. And I thought, "Okay, I probably should give this a shot permanently."

That's what gave me a taste of being my own boss, and I did that for nine years. I really liked being my own boss. I liked being able to do the different aspects of the business because it was more interesting.

I think what drove me originally was that I loved what I was doing. When I started LinkedIn training, I thought, "Ooh, pandemic's hit. Need a different way to make some money because my business has been affected." Firstly, the motivation was survival, that was it. I had no clients because none of them could see their own clients and they were not generating work for me. I needed to survive, to make money.

But then I thought, "Hold on. This is changing people's lives. That sounds really worthy." What I was teaching people was helping them to get more clients and make their businesses more successful. And I was like, "This feels really good." Having this direct feedback from people saying, "This has been a total game-changer. I feel much more able to talk about this. I've opened up loads, and it's been a real change in my personal life as well as my business."

I thought, "Wow. What I'm doing is actually having far greater impact than I'd intended." All I was planning to do is help them to learn how to use LinkedIn better, but it was having more significant effects for people. Not everyone, but a lot of people, and that felt good. It dawned on me that I was actually doing something that was making a genuine difference to people. I was meeting new people and I was having fun doing it. I was able to be myself and be quirky and fun and silly, and it was resonating with people.

I felt accepted in a way that I hadn't before. I'm not the kind of person that seeks acceptance because I don't really care. But when I started finding other people who could relate to me, that felt good as well. It was giving me that dopamine hit constantly. It's all nice having a viral post or whatever, but that's irrelevant. It's the DMs when people say, "Something you said really changed how I look at things." Someone said this morning, "You posted something about your other income streams, and I started doing something similar off the back of your post. And I've made another 900 pounds on top of my wages in the last couple of months." I was like, "That's amazing." I mean, he just read one of my posts, started doing something he hadn't thought of, and makes this extra money for his family.

That was what became quite addictive. It's the impact that I can have, positive impact. I want to make a positive impact on people. And then when it started to really work and I started to build confidence, the driver has been that building in confidence for me. I want to see how far this can go. Because all of this is having the most incredible positive impact on my life and my son's life. I mean, being able to buy a house, which I never thought I'd be able to do, and securing his future. And hopefully being able to send him to a really good school when he gets to secondary school. That for me is, holy crap. That makes it all worth it.

If I'm being really honest, he's not my driver. Yes, I can give him an amazing life, but I can give him a happy life either way. Rich or poor. We were a very happy family before. I was stressed with paying bills, but we were happy. And I wouldn't say that having more money has made us happier as a family, because we are always happy. We adore each other, we make time for each other, and we are super close. The money's nice, but it's not the driver. The driver is how it makes me feel about myself and my abilities and wanting to explore the boundaries of my potential. And see how far I can go, because I never believed I could, and now I feel like I've just trained as an astronaut.

I'd say, being totally honest, it's that. I just want to see what I'm capable of. Because people seem to think I'm capable of more and more and more that I don't believe or that I haven't really thought of.

Sam Eaton:

I love that. Yeah, because it's always that how far you can go. And someone gave me this analogy, and I only realized it recently, that you can't eat an elephant in one sitting. And it's so true. Early on in a business, we all try and do everything. You're my client, you're my client, you're my client, you're my client. Stop, just stop, and work out exactly who they are.

When you get to that point and it's like, "Okay, I want to see how far I can go," each step of the way you're realizing, "Okay, now I've done this. Now I'll do that." And that elephant analogy really comes into play.

Lea Turner:

It's almost like for me it's a game. I've got this video game and I've discovered that actually I'm really quite good at it. The money is just the points that I'm collecting. And it's nice I can buy things that are helpful to get me better at the game and to make the game easier. But ultimately, the game is what I'm excited about. Because it's all these puzzle pieces. I need to hire someone to do that, and I've got this, this, and this all needs to be done this week. And if I slot that into there, that's going to make me this many extra points.

I'm a really logical person and I love a challenge, but because I've got ADHD as well, I need those constant dopamine hits. I need that constant stimulation. Running my own business and all of these different things, people say, "Oh, you are doing so many different things at once." I know, because I know I can do them, and I love it. And I know that a lot of people will say, "You can't focus on too many things because that's the recipe for success." I'm like, "Yeah, but you're not me, because that's how I thrive."

That brings that dopamine up for me. And it's a constant high. I think, "Okay, cool. I've got to get this done." And that extra pressure, especially when I'm short on time, makes the dopamine hit bigger because I'm like, "Yeah, I did it. And I got there just in time." Whoosh, I feel that rush. I feel like that it is just this game that I've just learned that I'm really good at, and I'm constantly learning the next move and the next skill that I need to level up to the next thing.

It genuinely comes naturally. A lot of the skills with the marketing stuff, I just know what to do through what I've learned from other people, and then put together to work for my audience and my people. I'm good at reading people and what they want and what they'll react to. Yeah, I mean my main driver is me. Because Dex would be happy either way. Yes, I can create a better future, but Dex would thrive because he's that kind of kid. And he's like me. I thrived when I was poor, and I'll thrive more as I earn more. But he doesn't need that. He just needs a mommy who loves him and sets a good example by working hard and supporting him.

And so really, it's finally finding something I'm truly passionate about, truly good at, that truly helps people and has a positive impact. And makes me feel fulfilled.

Sam Eaton:

Say someone's picking up this book and they're looking for real inspiration. They're at that horrid stage where it's just like, "Oh, oh, oh." Right on the precipice. They've got a half load of mates over here going, "You're mad," and the other half going, "Do it." And you're looking down the barrel of a potential business going, "I don't know where to start." What advice would you give them?

Lea Turner:

A mentor. I think if this person's not already using LinkedIn, LinkedIn was my place that I went to start seeing people that weren't very different from me, that were doing what I wanted to do, and were achieving what I wanted to achieve. And the mates that were going, "You're crazy," they didn't get it because they earn a wage, and they get their wage in their pocket every month. But their earning potential is finite. I don't want a finite earning potential. I want to, if I need more money, I can just go and make more money. And to know that that's a possibility because that brings your confidence up a lot, being able to have the freedom and ability to do that.

You need to surround yourself with people who go, "You're not crazy. You can do this." That will be the biggest thing. Get yourself onto a social media platform and connect with and follow the content of people who are a few steps ahead of you, or even a lot of steps ahead of you. They represent what you can do in the short-term and what you can do in the long-term.

A lot of them will act as mentors in their own way, even if it's not directly. I found a lot of mentoring content that's made me go, "Oh, actually, hadn't thought about that. And that's a really good idea. And yeah, I really do that, or I should stop that." And I've learned a lot just from that. Read, read lots of books, watch videos, and listen to podcasts of people as well that are in the entrepreneurial world.

Decide if the biggest thing is the risk in trying and failing or in never trying and staying exactly where you are. Because for me, people say, "Oh my God, that's such a big risk. Such a big risk that you're moving to New Zealand and giving up everything you have here. It's such a big risk that you're going to have a baby on your own. It's such a big risk that you're going to travel to all these places on your own." But the risk for me is not doing those things, staying in my comfort zone, and never exploring what's possible.

The most common thing that people say on their deathbed is that they regret living their life for somebody else. Other people will say, "You should do this, you should be this. This is the kind of things that should make you happy." But you can't do that, otherwise you're going to be lying on your deathbed wishing that you hadn't. Wondering what could have been possible if you've just done this. And so for me, there is no risk in trying and failing. Failing means you tried, and that's a lot more than most people do. So don't fear failure. Fear living a life of mediocrity where you never try for more and believe you deserve more.

For me, that's what made me go, "I have a viable business. I could stay exactly where I am, and things will stay exactly as they are for the next however many years. Or I could give it a shot and try for more." And it's a no-brainer, really, isn't it? It doesn't matter what other people say if they think you're crazy, because those same people will be going, "Oh wow. How did you do that?"

Five years down the line, when you're absolutely killing it, raking in millions, and doing all the things that make you passionate and happy, they're going to be going, "Oh, you're so lucky." They're the same people that called you crazy for doing it. They will never do anything outstanding in their lives, they just won't. That's not their mentality.

I'm accidentally speaking in inspirational quotes there.

Sam Eaton:

Love that.

43

How to Communicate Successfully

"In many ways, effective communication begins with mutual respect, communication that inspires, encourages others to do their best."
~Zig Ziglar

I felt stupid. I sat round a dinner table with friends, one of whom had just got a new job. They described what they did, and everyone nodded and congratulated them.

"Can you explain what you are doing again?" I asked. "I'm so sorry, I just don't understand."

The table fell silent, all eyes on me. My face flushed with embarrassment and then my friend tried again. I still didn't get it, and I started to ask more questions. It turns out that they were going to be a head-hunter. The language they used to describe what they were doing was such that I just didn't get it. In fact, quite a few of us felt the same. I was the only one who asked the questions.

The same goes for websites. How often do you open a website, but you are left none the wiser on what they do after reading it? No idea, in fact! Why couldn't they just say what they do and the benefits of working with them rather than using industry jargon?

As your business grows, it's a common trap to fall into. What can you do to avoid that pitfall?

When you explain what you do, keep the industry jargon out of it. Be you. I'll give you an example:

"I am an HR consultant that specialises in organisational design using the Congruence Model."

OR:

"I can help you to plan who you need in your business and when you'll need them through careful planning that helps build your team to have the right skills at the right time."

See the difference?

There will be other times when you think you and your audience are communicating well, and that's simply not the case.

During the launch of the interactive platform I worked for, we were invited into a leading and exclusive fashion house.

Our team explained more about the benefits of interactive television and how it worked from a consumer perspective, and we invited journalists and editors to come up to the presentation area to use the system. One of the editors asked how many satellite dishes they'd need to install.

We were horrified! Just horrified! They only needed one for the TV viewing and the interactive platform. How on earth had we given them the perception that they needed more than one satellite dish?

Was it funny? Absolutely! The part that wasn't so funny is we were so caught up in our world and language that we forgot we were presenting a totally new concept. Why should they have thought any differently?

I use a simple philosophy these days: when I'm trying to explain a business concept to someone I have just met, who has nothing to do with that industry, I ask myself, "Does my description of that business make sense? Is it obvious what we do?" If it isn't, then it's back to the drawing board to make it clearer.

Write down what you do and consider the questions that I posed above. Who can you share it with to get feedback? Give yourself a score of 1-10 and ask the person reviewing it to rate you. One is poor and it's unclear what you do, and ten means they absolutely understand what you do and the benefits of working with you.

This approach can work across many areas of your business as you grow and evolve. At times, that evolution will be faster than others. That's where clarity can be so useful.

44

Beware the Time-Wasters

and Thieves

"Perspective is as simple as answering this question:
If I had 5 months to live, would I experience this problem differently?"
~Shannon L. Alder

Congratulations! Your business is beginning to grow. You are getting busier with clients, new team members, keeping ON the business, and on top of what needs doing.

Before you know it, a day can become disruptive.

- Too many phone calls—some of which are unexpected.

- Social media is a real distraction.

- Unnecessarily long meetings.

- Not enough time to delegate, which leads to projects slowing down.

Can you put your phone on silent and/or take important calls during certain times of the day? As we've touched on in earlier chapters, create 'power hours' to work exclusively on your social media. By splitting your time in the day to focus on it, you will continue to grow your audience without it becoming a distraction.

Unnecessarily long meetings can include initial calls with prospects. The golden rule is to keep your first connection call to around twenty minutes and ask the defining questions that will help you to establish if they are an ideal client for you. If at the end of that time, you establish they are not a good fit, you've invested twenty minutes as opposed to a whole hour.

Can you utilise platforms such as WhatsApp in different ways to stay connected with the team? We use the voice app all the time across our team. It really helps us to ask real-time questions and respond quickly.

As your business grows, so does the workload. This is where you have more things to juggle. Continuously work on your things-to-do list and challenge yourself on what you can delegate and fast.

The frustration will come if you need to coach people on how to do something, particularly if it's a new skill that person doesn't have yet. Invest that time by preparing well for any handover meeting in which you are explaining something new that you want them to do. It will help prevent a plethora of questions.

This is something to be mindful of and keep more front of mind as your business grows. Should I really be doing this? What is the cost to the business of my doing this? Are we better served if I pass this to someone else? Who should that be?

It's probably a good idea to talk about one of the biggest risks to any business owner: burnout.

Let's look at that next.

45

Burnout

*"Balance is the epiphany that you don't have to
be everything to everyone, all of the time."*
~Vanessa Autrey

I've opened, closed, opened, and closed again a blank page on this. A subject I know all too well. Why is that? Why couldn't I just write about it?

All the times I've made myself sick, or rather allowed myself to become sick, because I told myself "I had to…" or "I must…"

Maybe I'm ashamed I let myself get to that point. Maybe it's pride, or too much of it?

Sound familiar?

Let's face it, as business owners—or in fact, as driven individuals as whole—most of us have experienced burnout at one point or another in our lives and appreciate how crippling it can become as our minds and bodies do what they need to do to protect us and help us heal.

When we hear the big stats, research has shown that workplace stress impacts health and, sadly, mortality. It costs up to $190 billion each year, according to some reports, and up to $500 billion according to others. The bottom line is that, behind every stat, there's a person, there's a family, there's someone who cares.

Working an average of sixteen hours per day, five day a week (or sometimes six) isn't healthy. I'll accept that—in fact, I *know* that. It's all about managing me and taking the time to look after me.

There are several things that are imperative to preventing burnout.

Firstly, sleep. It's underrated by so many of us. Former PepsiCo Chairperson and CEO Indra Nooyi gets four hours a night, as does Martha Stewart. The famous fashion designer Tom Ford allegedly gets even less than that, three hours a night.

I've learnt the hard way that sleep isn't something we can 'bank.' I follow Dr. Matthew Walker, a sleep expert and a professor of neuroscience. He literally wrote the book on sleep: *Why We Sleep.* In it, he discusses the fact that, if we are sleep deprived, even if we are able to sleep and recover that night's deprivation, we can never get that night's sleep back.

If we don't get enough sleep, it affects our hormones, affects our performance, increases our anxiety levels, and is detrimental to our mental health.

Putting on weight has been a huge battle for me. I've put it down to being post-menopausal. However, I've also realised that I haven't been helping myself either. Not drinking enough water, doing the wrong exercises, and eating the wrong foods at the wrong times. For example, I've spent years having a protein shake in the morning. I've scrapped that for a mixture of eggs, feta cheese, smoked salmon, fresh chives, spinach, and chilies for breakfast. It sounds appetising, doesn't it? Well, let me tell you, it's amazing.

That breakfast has fuelled many a morning. Together with a healthy lunch and light supper, I have obliterated the late afternoon drowsiness dip and have improved my performance.

Burnout is a terrible thing. Planning our daily 'Me Time' and making it compulsory is essential. You can also mix in short bursts of exercise, naps, and healthy snacks to balance out your workday. All so obvious right? All so easy to overlook in the pursuit of ambition. I even put time in my diary to shower and get ready in the morning. Every bit of my day is planned. It helps me to stay organised, keep focused, and stay in control. That control keeps me healthier for the long haul.

"YOU are the most important asset you have." I have said many times throughout this book. You must practice self-care in order to build a successful business.

46

Contingency Budgets

*"A personal budget is a manifestation of your decision
to grab your finances by the balls."*
~Money Tree Man

By definition, a contingency budget is an emergency fund and is there for those unexpected costs. There will always be a few surprises along the way, a bit like running a home—just with greater ramifications.

Building a business is no mean feat. It takes long hours, focus, a ton of resilience, and self-reflection for those tough decisions. So what I'm going to say might seem like a pipedream right now.

Being on top of your finances is critical, and obvious. What if I suggested having six months' worth of costs and salary for you in the bank?

That is where I like to get my clients to over time, and it *does take time* to get to that stage.

Reaching that milestone will help to alleviate the pressure on you to get in every single penny or dime. It helps you get past that pressure to accept all clients—even the ones you *know* are a bad match for you in the first place.

It's tough, really tough, to say no to potential revenue, to say no to real money coming in while you are building your business and leads can be scarce. It feels counterintuitive. However, saying no to those that are clearly not right for you will help you to focus on finding those clients that are.

In turn, this will help you feel more comfortable in the sales process and help you to close that business with enthusiasm.

How do you go about creating a contingency plan? First, identify a list of your priority resources. It could be software, hardware, office equipment, etc.

Really make sure you have considered the potential risks, or as many as you possibly can, such as inflation, geo-politics, and risks that are outside of your control that might have impact. Once you've got a list of these risks, it will be a worthy exercise to develop strategies on how you will deal with them.

As you are building cash in the business and your contingency budget, can you find a line of credit? Some business owners prefer to self-fund.

Good planning will help you to plan, grow, and protect your business. A plan evolves, just like your business.

And the good news is that with growth comes the ability to be able to build that contingency budget.

47

The End – or Is It?

"The type of person you are is usually reflected in your business. To improve your business, first improve yourself."
~Idowu Koyenikan

Well, gosh, this has been interesting. I hope you've enjoyed reading about how others have built their businesses, sharing their wisdom, their highs and lows.

Ultimately, building a business is about people—it always has been and always will be. Even with the advent of AI, especially with the advent of AI, people will still come first.

Most of the time, business is a logical practice. People's opinions and emotions can get in the way of that all too often. Anyway, enough of that. Great communication and listening without judgement will be a skill that you learn to develop over time as a business owner.

I'm pretty sure if you were to ask most business owners (myself included), there's a lot they don't know. That's why I also invest heavily in my own development and coaching.

Running a business isn't meant to be easy. After all, if it were, surely everyone would do it. Where would the likes of the big beasts such as Amazon and Google be today if that were the case?

A business is a way of life. It annoys me when I read 'experts' encouraging people to leave their full-time, well-paid, guaranteed monthly income to have 'freedom.' Let me tell you, running your own business doesn't give you freedom. Far from it. In the first few years, it's your life as you build the income to replace your previous full-time salary and hopefully eclipse that.

I've got to share a funny story with you that I heard only this morning and made a mental note to include it in my last chapter.

Don't be fooled by what you read on social media. Did you know that a lot of these 'influencers' you see on private jets have their photos taken in a hangar of a plane on the ground? In fact, recently, one such influencer took a photo of themselves in front of a sleek jet and was spotted and photographed moments later getting onto a commercial flight. Madness! Pure madness! Personally, I think that's deceitful smoke and mirrors—harsh, I know. I want people to really understand that this isn't easy. Yes, it's rewarding. Yes, it's fun. And it's a very steep learning curve each and every day.

What a business does give you is flexibility to work when you want to. So many of my clients love the fact they can pick up and drop off their children most days. They are there for bedtime, even if they are then working until the small hours of the following day whilst the kids are sleeping.

It isn't for everyone, and that's okay too.

However, running your own business is exceptionally rewarding. I get such a kick out of seeing my clients paying for family holidays because they've been able to take on staff. In fact, one of my clients has just come back from St Lucia, having booked and paid for it out of her earnings that she is now able to pay herself.

Another one of my clients has just purchased a house, outright, for her growing family.

Earlier, I explained that my goal is to help founders build success on their terms. They expect me to work with them to get more sales and increase margins. It's the other stuff, like building their teams, increasing profitability per head, and coaching them to be great at what they do, that makes me a little bit different.

My absolute, unrelenting, unwavering desire to make a difference is what has made us successful and will continue to make us successful over the next few years.

I have loved sharing with you honestly and wholeheartedly what works and what hasn't worked. I hope it helps you to continue your path to success, wherever that may lead.

I would love to hear your stories, share in your successes, and answer questions.

Please find me on LinkedIn:

linkedin.com/in/SamanthaEaton1450